Religion and Change

European Academy of Religion (EuARe) Lectures

EuARe Executive Committee:
Karla Boersma, Francesca Cadeddu, Jocelyne Cesari,
Silvio Ferrari, Vincente Fortier, Hans-Peter Grosshans,
Pantelis Kalaitzidis, Frederik Pedersen,
Herman J. Selderhuis

Volume 4

Religion and Change

Fourth Annual Conference 2021

Edited by
Hans-Peter Grosshans

DE GRUYTER

Published with the financial support of the Seminar for Systematic Theology and the Institute for Ecumenical Theology of the Faculty of Protestant Theology of the University of Münster (Germany).

ISBN 978-3-11-124102-9
e-ISBN (PDF) 978-3-11-124146-3
e-ISBN (EPUB) 978-3-11-124177-7
DOI https://doi.org/10.1515/9783111241463
ISSN 2940-455X

This work is licensed under the Creative Commons Attribution 4.0 International License.
For details go to https://creativecommons.org/licenses/by/4.0/.

Library of Congress Control Number: 2023907132

Bibliographic information published by the Deutsche Nationalbibliothek
The Deutsche Nationalbibliothek lists this publication in the Deutsche Nationalbibliografie; detailed bibliographic data are available on the Internet at http://dnb.dnb.de.

© 2023 with the author(s), editing © Hans-Peter Grosshans, published by Walter de Gruyter GmbH, Berlin/Boston. This book is published with open access at www.degruyter.com.
Printing and binding: CPI books GmbH, Leck

www.degruyter.com

Contents

Hans-Peter Grosshans
Introduction —— 1

Rowan Williams
Tradition, Traditionalism, and Culture Wars —— 5

Judith Wolfe
Reading the Signs of the Times: Theology and the Question of Progress —— 25

Vassilis Saroglou
Sameness, Adaptation, or Change? Understanding the Specifics and Limits of Religious Change —— 39

Guy G. Stroumsa
The Study of Religion and the Spirit of Orientalism: Cultural Transformations and Scholarly Shifts —— 63

Azza Karam
Complimenting the Divine: The Multireligious as the Poetics of Resilience —— 77

Contributors —— 89

Index of Persons —— 91

Hans-Peter Grosshans
Introduction

This volume of essays documents the five keynote lectures at the 2021 Annual Congress of the *European Academy of Religion (EuARe)*, which took place from 30 August – 2 September 2021 at the University of Münster (Germany) on the theme of 'Religion and Change'.

The theme of 'change' was unmistakable at this congress. Due to the SARS-CoV-2 virus pandemic, the congress had to be held in a hybrid format, so that three hundred people physically attending in Münster could unite with five hundred online participants to form a discourse community. Just as the scientific community has faced change as a result of the pandemic, religious communities have also faced multiple changes in the years of the SARS-Cov-2 virus pandemic since 2020. New formats of religious life, cooperation and communication had to be tested. Traditional forms of meeting and cultic events in religious communities were now seen as risk situations and had to be changed. Traditional rituals could only be practised to a limited extent or not at all. The religious communities mostly reacted creatively to the pandemic situation with variations of the usual and with new formats, especially digital ones. The topic of 'religion and change' had a pressing topicality for all religious communities during the SARS-CoV-2 virus pandemic – and often in the context of an authoritarian, immobile and downright pre-modern stately pandemic management.

However, religious communities have not only been dealing with the issue of change since the SARS-Cov-2 virus pandemic. Even pandemics in earlier times have often led to changes in the practice of religious communities, just as many other significant social events have led to changes in religious communities' doctrine and practice. It is a question repeatedly examined with regard to concrete religious communities whether and how religious communities reacted to very significant changes in society, culture and politics and whether these changes left their mark on their doctrine and practice and led to their change. In addition, however, the topic of religion and change is also about longer-term processes of change in religious communities and, above all, about the possibilities for change inherent in the religious communities structurally and doctrinally.

Looking generally at the religious system, e.g. in Europe, in historical perspective, continuous changes are evident. The religious map of Europe has become more diverse and colourful in the last half century – as in many other parts of the world. Practically all religions of the world are increasingly present in Europe. This is part of a change in religion (in the singular) in Europe that has been taking place for some time.

In the history of European religion, Christianity was able to establish itself from the 3rd century onwards. Along with Judaism, it is one of the two religions that have been continuously present throughout European history over the last 2000 years. From the Middle Ages onwards, Islam had a regional presence in Europe. In modern times, the situation changed insofar as other religions became present – often covertly at first. An intensive preoccupation with non-Christian religions began among scholars and writers, especially with Islam and its poetry, but also with Indian, Chinese and Japanese texts. Hindu-Buddhist thought, and to some extent Confucian thought, made its way into Europe and was also reflected in the founding of societies – think of anthroposophy (Rudolf Steiner), for example. In the 20th century, elements and practices (such as meditation) of non-Christian religions were positively received in European Christianity. Due to colonialism and later due to global migration movements, there is increased immigration of Hindus, Buddhists, Sikhs and Muslims to Europe from the 19th century onwards. By the end of the 20th century, there was a considerable increase in people of non-Christian religious affiliation in Europe, resulting in multi-religious and multi-cultural societies. Today, almost all religious traditions are present in many major European cities: Muslim mosque associations, Hindu temple communities, Buddhist pagoda communities, Sikh gurdwara communities, African and Indian traditions, the so-called youth religions, esoteric groups, etc. contribute to religious life in Europe's major cities alongside Christian and Jewish communities. The overall situation of religion in Europe is itself in a permanent state of change. This is reinforced by the fact that the individual religions also have a dynamic internal history of pluralisation through denominations, schools and directions.

This change in the religious map of Europe has also become generally aware in the public, at the latest with the migrations to Europe in recent decades, and can no longer be ignored even by the supporters of the secularisation theory in all its varieties. At the same time, the question arises as to the adaptability not only of religiously influenced people, but especially of religions as a whole to the modern world that characterises contemporary Europe. This then also raises the question of the extent to which religions can change at all.

For some people, their religion is the only stable element in a world of permanent change, as it relates them to something that is transcendent to this world and therefore unaffected by change. But is this really true? Is the transcendent really beyond and without change? And are religions, even if they refer people to an unchanging transcendence, then also unchanging or not rather themselves subject to change like everything else in the world?

In most religions, long-standing traditions with their practices and their sacred texts are of paramount importance, and fidelity to these traditions and texts seems to give the religions the character of immutability. At the same time, all religions

– in varying degrees and forms – have a rich practice of interpreting their sacred texts and books, as well as their ritual practices and all activities within religious practice in general. Often – sometimes downright counter-intuitively – the emphasis on traditions or the original meaning of texts is the basis for changes in religions. How can these hermeneutical processes be described and how are they related to the change within religions and the change in society caused by religions?

At the 2021 Congress of the *European Academy of Religion* in Münster, these general questions on the topic of 'Religion and Change' should be discussed in four ways in the five keynote lectures, the three central discussions or the more than 170 panels: 1. with regard to the change and transformation of religion in general in the history of religions; 2. with regard to the relationship between evolution and religion; 3. with regard to a hermeneutics adequate to religious traditions, texts and practices; 4. with regard to the general dynamics of change inherent in religions with regard to themselves, but especially also to their social, cultural and political contexts.

The academic objective of the congress was thus at least twofold: firstly, to discuss and deepen the topic of 'Religion and Change' in an inter- and transdisciplinary discourse and against the background of different religious and confessional traditions; secondly, to bring into discourse with each other different areas of religious research with their respective methodological peculiarities and perspectives, but also their anchoring in and allocation to different religious, confessional, cultural and linguistic traditions in the history of the humanities.

The five main papers presented here in revised form in this volume exemplify the treatment of the topic of 'Religion and Change' at the Congress. I am very grateful to Rowan Williams, Judith Wolfe, Vasilis Saroglou, Guy G. Stroumsa and Azza Karam for making their contributions available for this publication. I would also like to thank Albrecht Döhnert and the publishing house De Gruyter for the opportunity to publish in a new series, in which the keynote lectures of the congresses of the *European Academy of Religion* will be documented in the future. As former president of the *European Academy of Religion*, I would like to thank all those who supported me in this task during the time of the pandemic, especially in the organisation and implementation of the congress and also in the preparation of this publication. On behalf of all these supportive people, I would like to make special mention here of my research assistants Lena Mausbach, Micha Kuhn and Jan Turck.

Rowan Williams
Tradition, Traditionalism, and Culture Wars

1

One of the themes that emerged in different forms and in different places in the philosophy of the second half of the 20th century was the recognition that 'meaning' is a social project and a social product. Wittgenstein's famous dismantling of the idea of a private language – still quite commonly misunderstood as a simple attack on the idea of interiority itself – is no more than an analysis of how we cannot decide for ourselves what *counts* as a valid, recognizable move in our speech; even if we are 'talking to ourselves', we have to posit continuities and structures, whose only possible source is the structured language we are always already hearing as participants in a linguistic world. From a very different intellectual standpoint, the defence of tradition – and even of 'prejudice' – by Hans-Georg Gadamer insisted that the skills of understanding were always *learned*: to be inducted into any active human exchange is to absorb perspectives that are taken for granted, pre-judgments that we as individuals do not construct for ourselves.[1] To put it succinctly, we cannot teach ourselves to speak; and if that is the case, then there is always in our claims to knowing and understanding an irreducible element of *dependence*. We are born into a process we have not initiated. We may stand back from it, critique it, seek to change its protocols and boundaries, but we cannot begin without it. Grasping this is grasping that – at the very least – any kind of social agency, any human activity that is necessarily shared, requires that words and gestures be mutually recognizable, that we know what counts as a move in the game, what is likely to produce a response that is intelligible in turn to me as speaker and so continues to enable collaborative action. That we talk with each other and that we identify actions that can only be performed in collaboration are inseparably part of what has to be said about human identity as such; and both point to the inescapability of learning a 'grammar' of action, and acknowledging that our emergence as human agents – which includes our emergence as self-reflective subjects capable of *scrutinizing* and revising what we say – assumes a structured world of meaning. John Haldane puts it neatly:

---

[1] Hans-Georg Gadamer, *Truth and Method*. Translation ed. Joel Weisheimer and Donald C. Marshall. London/New York (NY): Continuum ²1989.

> The very idea that we can conceive of ourselves as agents entering into a scheme of political association independently of knowing ourselves (however inarticulately) to have a particular, socially-constituted nature is incoherent. As incoherent, indeed, as supposing that one could think of oneself as entering into a commercial transaction as a banker independently of locating oneself within a pre-existing order of financial exchange.[2]

What is more, we learn this 'socially-constituted nature' by a variety of means, many of them more or less tacit. We pick up cues from custom and story, from what T.S. Eliot called 'forms of festivity'[3], the rhythms of a calendar, even the conventions of a cuisine,[4] just as much as from explicit instruction in ideals or proprieties. And in this connection, it is clear enough that learning how to understand is precisely *not* a matter of absorbing universal rules of reasoning: circles of recognition and recognisability gradually widen, press at their boundaries, advance or retreat, in and through the contingent tensions of actual encounter. Think of the common experience of discovering how to decode physical gestures in an unfamiliar setting: what is a harmless hand movement in one setting turns out to be seriously offensive in another; a shake of the head may indicate assent in one context and negation in another. A recognizable 'grammar' comes to light only gradually, as a result of attention and willingness to spend time being taught.

All this is to say that if the notoriously slippery word 'culture' has a central area of definition, it has something to do with these *meanings we do not make for ourselves*, Gadamer's 'prejudices'; and 'tradition' is the process of transmitting such meanings, the pedagogy of recognition. As Gadamer and his followers have been at pains to underline, this has nothing to do with somehow privileging inherited wisdom over innovative thinking. It is a serious intellectual warning against the fantasy that we can definitively locate a thinking-place free from pre-judgement and the givenness of certain social determinants. Effective and adequate interpretation begins with the acknowledgement of this, with a self-questioning that informs our questioning of the system we stand in.[5] In slightly different terms, we need to be aware of what it is in what we have received that allows (or indeed mandates) the challenge we may put to that received set of meanings; our critique is never generated or delivered from 'nowhere', from a given or self-evident territory of universal rationality.

---

[2] John Haldane, *Practical Philosophy. Ethics, Society and Culture*. Exeter: Imprint Academic 2009, 279.
[3] Thomas S. Eliot, *Notes Towards the Definition of Culture*. London: Faber and Faber 1948, 16, n.1.
[4] Thomas S. Eliot, *Definition of Culture*, e.g. 51.
[5] Hans-Georg Gadamer, *Truth and Method*, 305–341, esp. 320–325.

The last seventy-odd years in philosophy have thus left us with a rehabilitation of tradition in some quarters, at least to the extent of a radical questioning of certain myths of universal rationality. Alasdair MacIntyre's vastly influential work[6] has familiarized the English-speaking world with the conceptual weaknesses of such mythologies and made a powerful case for rethinking our theories of knowledge and reasoning so as to do better justice to the material and historical inheritance of reasoning practices. But does this mean we are left with no general criteria for what counts as reasoning itself? Pope Benedict XVI argued on several occasions[7] that the malaise of modern Europe was largely to do with the abandonment of an ideal of reason that transcended cultural specificity or partisan interest; does the rehabilitation of tradition condemn us to relativism? Is the price of a new seriousness about tradition and inherited belonging an opening of the door to a chaos of identity politics and a comprehensive postmodern pluralism – with the unwelcome implication that stability can come only by way of victory in a contest of coercive power? The current era of 'culture wars' and assiduously-fostered scepticism about public truth is one in which we might well wonder whether the retrieval of tradition simply entrenched and canonized a violent tribalism. In this lecture, I hope to suggest that this negative conclusion is not the only way of reading the possibilities opened up by the philosophies of Gadamer or MacIntyre. Paul Ricœur's analysis of the debates about tradition and reason suggests another perspective and a way back to some sort of 'universalism' about the human condition; and a family of theological reflections on tradition can fill this out further, helping us to see that the contemporary configurations of what tradition and culture mean have to be questioned very seriously. And understanding the flaws in these contemporary configurations may help us see that certain modern appeals to tradition are part of the problem rather than the solution in recovering what 'tradition' once meant and why it matters.

---

6 Alasdair MacIntyre, *After Virtue*. Notre Dame (IN): University of Notre Dame Press 1981 and Alasdair MacIntyre, *Whose Justice? Which Rationality?* Notre Dame (IN): University of Notre Dame Press 1988. To Alasdair MacIntyre, *Ethics and Politics. Selected Essays, Volume 2*. Cambridge: Cambridge University Press 2006.
7 Most famously and notoriously in the 'Regensburg address' of 2006; see James V. Schall, *The Regensburg Lecture*. South Bend (IN): St Augustine's Press 2007.

2

In 1973, Paul Ricœur published two substantial essays, overlapping a good deal in their argumentation: an article on 'Ethics and Culture'[8] and a somewhat better known and longer piece on 'Hermeneutics and the Critique of Ideology'[9]. Taken together, they offer a particularly acute and suggestive intervention in the Gadamer-Habermas debate about the relation of tradition and critique – or rather the relation between two idioms of philosophical analysis, one conceiving the philosophical task as essentially the 'participatory' taking forward of an always presupposed human conversation, the other insisting on the priority of exposing the distortions that routinely and covertly pervade and frustrate universal communication.[10] Of special interest for the subject we are looking at here is Ricœurs parsing of what underlies the 'critique' idiom, the exposure of *interests* which undermine claims to straightforward truthtelling. Ricœur summarizes[11] Habermas's identification of the three kinds of interest that are at work in human claims to knowledge. 'Instrumental interest' is the particular kind of selectivity that operates in our reading of our environment so as to deliver effective control over the ambient processes within which human agency occurs. 'Practical interest' is to do with how we set out to acquire a knowledge that will enable the communication of norms and expectations, the maintenance of certain sorts of human continuity in a way that allows those involved in the exchange to 'own' for themselves the ongoing processes of society at whatever level. In academic terms, these two interests correspond roughly to the work of the natural sciences and the traditional humanities, and there is no great gulf between Gadamerian and Habermasian accounts thus far.

---

8 Paul Ricœur, Ethics and Culture. Habermas and Gadamer in Dialogue, in: Paul Ricœur *Political and Social Essays*. Ed. David Stewart and Joseph Bien. Athens (OH): Ohio University Press 1974, 243–270.
9 Paul Ricœur, Hermeneutics and the Critique of Ideology, in: Paul Ricœur, *Hermeneutics and the Human Sciences*. Edited, translated and introduced by John B. Thomspon. Cambridge: Cambridge University Press 1981, 63–100. Some of the same territory is also covered in Paul Ricœur, Science and Ideology (originally published in 1974), in: Paul Ricœur, *Hermeneutics and the Human Sciences*, 222–246.
10 Paul Ricœur, Hermeneutics and the Critique, 99: 'The first [sc.hermeneutics]…is turned towards a consensus which precedes us and, in this sense, which exists; the second anticipates a future freedom in the form of a regulative idea which is not a reality but an ideal, the ideal of unrestricted and unconstrained communication.' Cf. the well-known exchanges between Gadamer and Habermas in the early 1970s; Jack Mendelson, The Habermas-Gadamer Debate, in: *New German Critique 18* (1979), 44–73, remains a useful overview, and see also Alan How, *The Habermas-Gadamer Debate and the Nature of the Social. Back to Bedrock*. Avebury 1995.
11 Paul Ricœur, Ethics and Culture, 254–257; cf. Paul Ricœur, Hermeneutics and the Critique, 80–83.

The key divergence comes with the identification of the third kind of interest, the 'emancipatory', which belongs to the critical social sciences. This is the interest that focuses on the ways in which power distorts communication: it is, you could say, an interest in the idea of 'interest' itself, 'interest' as the intrusion into communicative relationships of an agenda that has to do with advantage and privilege – ultimately with the control of other human agents, not only of environmental processes. It is generated 'at the same level where work, power and discourse are intertwined'[12]; and this is the complex of intellectual phenomena designated by the term 'ideology'.

Critical philosophy thus enjoins a *suspicion* of alleged consensus and inherited conceptualities; in relation to any claim about 'given' truths, it will ask *cui bono*? Whose interest is served? Modernity is generally predicated – with more and more explicitness – on the priority of this emancipatory questioning; it encourages us to see inherited thinking and custom, tradition, as no longer neutral. It is either a necessary support or

> a form of violence exercised against our thinking, which prevents us from advancing to maturity of judgement.[13]

The problem is that if we come to see what is inherited as intrinsically 'violent', we are left with the impossible imperative of constructing meanings that are untouched by dependence – which, strictly speaking, would entail meanings that were beyond language (Nietzsche said, we might recall, that God was not dead so long as we still used grammar...). If there is no legitimate authority anywhere, there is no reliable path of learning. And this leaves us with a human subject condemned to the godlike task of creation out of nothing; a godlikeness indistinguishable from total impotence.

This is not a sustainable intellectual position, and cannot be what Habermas, or critical philosophy in general, really intends; so Ricœur interrogates critique and emancipation a bit further. It does not make sense, he notes,[14] to try to

> explain without understanding: human interaction, crucially human linguistic/cultural interaction, is not an object whose mechanisms we can observe from outside. We cannot reduce emancipatory interest to some form of instrumental interest. Emancipation is an ethical ideal: it begins in a judgement of *value*, the value of human communication itself, and as such, it is significantly different from a valuation grounded in instrumental judgements of functional success or practical problem-solving.[15]

---

12 Paul Ricœur, Ethics and Culture, 255–256.
13 Paul Ricœur, Ethics and Culture, 246.
14 Paul Ricœur, Ethics and Culture, 265.
15 Paul Ricœur, Ethics and Culture, 266–267.

And that in turn entails a valuation of the *transmission* of perception, habit, and so on, the processes by which we are inducted into the sphere of mutual recognisability which is human community. Critique devoid of this valuation of transmitted understanding is 'empty and anemic', says Ricœur;[16] worse, it itself becomes an ideology, privileging the systematically repressive reign of functionalism, the tyranny of technological modernity. The regulative ideal of open communication which Habermas looks to is one that takes for granted that communication is a *human good*. Ideology is an ethical problem because it impedes active common life – because it impedes tradition, we might provocatively say. We know something of what 'communicative action' means, and so why it is important to resist what corrupts and limits it. And in the background is a point Ricœur does not make in any very explicit way, but which may turn out to be of significance for this discussion later on: communication is the means by which we are made actively human, and unrestricted communication is important because it allows the exchange of what a more overtly religious discourse would call gift and communion.

And the complementary insight that Ricœur notes in hermeneutical philosophy is that, characteristically, interpretation is not a simple process of unquestioning reception because its objects are – in the widest sense – 'textual'.[17] Traditions articulate themselves and become objects of reflection to themselves in the various symbolic codes in which they work and live. Meaning is distanced from individual authors or speakers, it is *mediated* in cultural production and so becomes a site for debate: the truth, rather than being a direct, unassailable presence, is something glimpsed, pointed to, contested, no less than it is affirmed and trusted. And the text (remembering that various forms of conscious and living communicative practice are included in the term) becomes a world into which the subject is invited so as to 'stake' and articulate a linguistic identity, a presence *as* subject by way of what Ricœur memorably designates as 'imaginative variations of the ego'[18]. The point is that the hermeneutical exercise is clearly involved in a kind of critical practice. The 'suspicious' critical subject is reminded that it is itself open to suspicion because it is located, addressed, 'invested' (to borrow Gillian Rose's favoured term), as it seeks to engage with other located and invested subjects; critique is turned on itself, not in a destructive way but in the sense that the critical subject has to come to terms with being both questioned and invited. We are close here to MacIntyre's insistence that a well-functioning tradition

---

16 Paul Ricœur, Ethics and Culture, 266.
17 Paul Ricœur, Hermeneutics and the Critique, 91–95; cf. Paul Ricœur, Ethics and Culture, 258–260.
18 Paul Ricœur, Hermeneutics and the Critique, 94.

is always partially constituted by an argument about the goods the pursuit of which gives to that tradition its particular point and purpose.[19]

Tradition, in communicating vision, perspective, priority, and so forth, in claiming authority to shape the understanding of new human situations as they arise, does not foreclose but generates argument because *it provides the tools for the speaking subject to act.* There is no interpretative practice that is not in some degree inflected by what Ricœur calls 'ethical distance' for what has been inherited.[20] This or that current formulation is being scrutinized for its adequacy in transmitting a life-giving truth, not simply repeated; and in the process, the subject determines and risks a specific place to speak from, which is not identical with any other.

The 'critical' subject is first (like every subject) a learner; the interpreting and participating subject is inescapably an innovator. Ricœur's contribution to the debate is to highlight two fundamental facts – that hermeneutics and critique belong on a spectrum, and that ethical and normative elements are built in to the discussion. The 'emancipatory' worry about distorting agendas is already present in hermeneutical practice if it knows its business, simply because the interpreter's investment in unimpeded and authentic transmission within a historical community requires a sharp ear for axes being ground that would fracture the community by privileging one part of it and silencing or disenfranchising another. If both the hermeneutical and the critical thinker assume that communal life is the essential context for the project of maturing human subjecthood, both are assuming an anthropology in which it matters supremely to attend to whatever unbalances and divides that communal life and entrenches inequalities of participation. A concern with tradition is likely to see such participation as in some ways intrinsically differentiated, even hierarchical, while the perspective of ideological critique will be more deeply invested in the ideal of undifferentiated access. There are major theoretical issues to be argued in this connection. But the key factor is the assumption of an irreducibly common human project; and, following on from that, such a formulation implies that a basic question about the health and (in the fullest sense) rationality of a society will be that of *trust*: the project into which we are invited is one that is meant to work in everyone's interest, in the sense at least that it is seen as what makes possible a just and appropriate share in common goods and common good.

Absent this anthropology it is impossible to assume trust. If we cannot take it for granted that either the specific human neighbour or the social institution can be

---

19 Alasdair MacIntyre, *After Virtue*, 206.
20 Paul Ricœur, Ethics and Culture, 268.

seen as invested in a common project whose aim is some sort of *shared* flourishing, the obvious imperative is to defend my interest against a potentially hostile neighbour or social institution. Ricœur, as we have seen, identified the instrumentalizing tendencies of technological and capitalist modernity as the prevailing ideological force of late modernity; nearly fifty years on from the writing of these essays, we can recognize his prescience, but might carry the analysis a bit further. The triumph of the instrumental interest has fostered a model of human subjecthood as a disconnected sequence of problematic needs to be met or gaps to be filled: the subject identifies a lack, and the system moves into operation to supply it. 'Consumerism' is one word for this, but perhaps too weak a designation, as the issue is not simply one of marketized commodities – or more accurately, perhaps, it is about the perception of any and every lack in terms of marketized commodities,[21] discrete, purchasable solutions to discrete kinds of wanting. Habermasian critique was envisaged as a scrutiny of social history, forces and phenomena that could lay bare interests which prevented critical participation in a common task; but how is it to cope with an ideology that assumes the irreducible conflict of interest to be the fundamental truth of social life?

3

If the social fabric overall fails to generate trust, people will look all the more eagerly for affiliations that will provide the context of mutual recognition which enables them to grow and thrive; affiliations whose relation to a wider social or global nexus will be varied, to put it mildly. This is the point at which – for example – nationalisms become not merely affirmations of the value and human resourcefulness of specific local inheritance but ideologies invested in heady dramas of innocence, purity, victimhood, and the like. The local, the particular, has to be not only valuable but beyond critique; and as such, it is considered as needing unquestioning and uncompromising defence against any suggestion that its history is morally shadowed (like other histories). The pattern is reproduced in many forms of identity politics when they move beyond the pressure for just reparation and inclusion into a territory where any uncertainty about the exact vehicles for such reparation and inclusion is seen as treachery and any questioning or delay is cast as actively and maliciously threatening. The effect of this is, inevitably, a further

---

[21] An influential recent discussion in Michael Sandel, *What Money Can't Buy. The Moral Limits of Markets*. New York (NY): Farrar, Strauss and Giroux 2012.

fragmenting of identity and an intensified hostility between different sub-groups within a marginal or subaltern population; an effect which can consolidate precisely the unjust or violent status quo which is being challenged.

And here is one of the central paradoxes that needs naming and considering. Faced with the twin problem of an instrumentalized public sphere, with the alienation attendant on it, and a Balkanized landscape of competing interests, there is a temptation to reach for a reaffirmation of 'tradition' that will once again connect individual lives and experiences with a common social project operating in accord with universal and unchallengeable law. But 'reaching for' a tradition is precisely what those inhabiting a tradition do not do; they *inherit* a perspective which they continue to accept as trustworthy; they do not survey a field of options and decide on one. 'Traditionalism' as an elective position is quintessentially modern in that it presupposes a prior distance from any specific traditional scheme. It becomes an ideology, a scheme of ideas and perspectives whose purpose is to defend a particular interest; as such, it is in part designed to tell you who can not be trusted or recognized. It must present itself as a conscious bid for certain sorts of power or liberty of expression, and so must also create the narrative of a disempowerment or repression against which it revolts (hence the enormous rhetorical weight of discourse around 'freedom of speech' in current debate). But to the extent that it sees fidelity to tradition as a *choice* whose possibility has to be secured, it presupposes that the subject – and the community of subjects – exists first in an indeterminate and contested space in which solidarity has to be created and its terms defined. This, though, is tantamount to saying that in certain crucial respects we can and do exist in a *pre-symbolic* context,[22] in that we need to articulate, define, and rationalize the *symbolique* by which we live and understand; and this is precisely the assumption that is made in the critique of tradition that has characterized so much of intellectual modernity. In other words, *the deliberate adoption of a tradition or the defence of a 'traditionalist' stance as one amongst others, accepts the premise of tradition-critique*. It is a mirror-image of what it purportedly refuses.

This does not mean that 'traditional' convictions or perspectives are impossible to hold in the contemporary intellectual world. As we shall see, a certain suspicion of self-conscious traditionalism generates some hermeneutical questions that leave open a number of constructive possibilities. But those possibilities will not come to light so long as we are held captive by the model of simple binary conflict between modernity and a tradition that is imagined as antithetical in every point to moder-

---

[22] See, for example, Paul Ricœur, Science and Ideology, in: Paul Ricœur, *Hermeneutics and the Human Sciences*. Edited, translated, and introduced by John B. Thomspon. Cambridge: Cambridge University Press 1981, 222–246, esp. 237–238.

nity. Dissolving this binary in the terms in which it is usually presented these days – dissolving the notion of a 'culture war' – involves some further thinking about a theme we have already touched on, the *learned* character of our convictions and the reflexive feedback that makes tradition an active and formative force. We have noted how Ricœur highlights those elements in the Gadamerian picture of tradition which emphasize that a living tradition continues to generate new problems for itself and is defined by a shared history of debate as much as by a set of fixed positions.[23] One of the oddest aspects of the current landscape of dramatic polarities is the failure to enquire about how new positions are actually arrived at and what authority they appeal to; and when such questions are pursued, the map will look rather different. A number of neuralgic problems will appear as conflicts internal to a shared discourse rather than a collision of self-contained intellectual worlds.

We can illustrate this by looking at some of the issues currently debated with a good deal of heat and often treated as tribal markers in the supposed culture wars. The bitter controversies over the rights of persons to determine their gender identity and to have a voice in shaping the social conventions that would guarantee recognition of their self-determination have brought to light a number of apparent polarities, not least among feminist theorists and advocates.[24] One strand of feminist thinking has resisted the case for regarding transgendered individuals as having the gender recognition in the public sphere that they argue for, on the grounds that the historic struggles of biologically female/cisgendered women for safe spaces in a threatening world of masculine dominance and violence are undermined by the creation of spaces that can be occupied by formerly male-identifying individuals. Some have also argued that the linking of gender to socially-sanctioned conventions of behaviour, dress, and so on reverses the historic feminist concern to *separate* gender from social convention and expectation and implies a reversion to the 'gender essentialism' that feminism historically sought to escape. At the same time, the movement for fuller recognition of transgendered – and non-binary – individuals has been opposed by more conservative voices arguing that the biological givenness of gender identity cannot be overturned by individual human choice; religious voices on this side of the debate have spoken about a repudiation of the fundamental order established by the Creator. In response, advocates of the recognition of gender-fluidity of various kinds have presented the case in terms of

---

23 Along with MacIntyre's comments on this, see the classic discussion by Walter B. Gallie, Essentially Contested Concepts, in: *Proceedings of the Aristotelian Society 56* (1956), 167–198.
24 A recent helpful overview of the social and practical, not only the 'ideological', issues is Ben Vincent, *Non-Binary Genders. Navigating Communities, Identities and Healthcare*. Bristol: Policy Press 2020.

two basic ethical concerns – the liberty of the individual to adopt whatever kind of public presence does not create unmanageable inner tension or cost, and the duty of society not only to accept the self-descriptions of minorities on their own terms rather than imposing roles and restrictions, but also to protect such minorities from demeaning and threatening speech or behaviour on the part of others.

What might strike someone reviewing the controversy is the degree to which it illustrates how a single discourse generates sharply diverse questions and conclusions. Feminism identifies at least two basic ethical concerns as essential to a just and participatory social order: no group or class of human beings should be at risk simply in virtue of their identity; and the biological givens of any individual's identity should not determine what is socially possible for them. The force of feminist argument, especially since the beginning of the last quarter of the last century, lay in the abundant demonstration of modern Western society's failure to honour these ethical concerns where women were concerned. But those concerns inexorably press further: what if the 'identity' in question is not straightforwardly and exhaustively correlated with the 'biological givens'? And what if the separation between biology and potential social role is – so to speak – reversible, so that the public performance of gender need not depend on original biological determination? Even as regards the religious criticism of gender-fluid discourse, the issues are not quite as completely clear as might be thought. The givenness of the body's identity and the acceptance of materiality have never been understood simply as a refusal of therapeutic interventions which seek to remedy profound tension or cost, to recall the terms used a little while ago; the case has to be made for regarding gender particularity as the one area in which no intervention is permissible or defensible to mitigate suffering.

The point is that the evolution of this debate shows the way in which moral traditions push at their own boundaries as the implications of how to implement the tradition become clearer over time. The fundamental convictions do not in fact alter; the disagreement is not about the principles but about whether this or that possible implementation so *undermines* the principle that it effectively moves into a different moral landscape. To take the most familiar objection to newer developments in this discussion, does the opening up of exclusively 'female' spaces (restrooms, female prisons) or opportunities (women's sports) to transgendered individuals undermine the hard-won protection of biologically female individuals? Or again, does the recognition of a self-identified (but not originally biologically female) woman somehow trivialise the specific physical constraints and struggles of the biologically female? But to cast the questions in those terms is to acknowledge that there is a set of goals that both parties can recognize; it does not prescribe an answer in general terms, but it permits a conversation to continue that does not assume a destructive or non-moral purpose on either side. By looking at the process by which people reach conclusions on the basis of recognizable principles, the debate can be configured as something other than a collision of completely alien moral universes. It may even be transformed into a debate about the actual resolution of *specific* challenges or injustices rather than a global war.

A second issue that could be analysed in a similar but distinct way is the question of immigration policy in the United Kingdom. Here too, the debate seems at first to be cast in the language of a competition between 'total' moralities, rival and mutually impervious systems – the vision of a hospitable society opposed to a nationalist and exclusive one; or the vision of a secure and manageable society opposed to an irresponsible and chaotic one, incapable of employing and caring for its own citizens and colluding with an economic model of disposable and mobile labour that is dehumanizing for all.[25] This instance is slightly more complicated than the first in one respect; whereas it would be hard to find a transgender advocate who actively wanted to eliminate biological difference or to sanction the humiliation of women, or a critic of gender fluidity who actively wanted to enshrine discrimination and legal penalties for people who have experienced transition of any kind, there really are opponents of more open immigration policies whose words and actions provide evidence of racism, crude 'cultural protectionism', and an allegiance to mythical and unhistorical pictures of national or ethnic purity. How conversation unfolds with such people is not exactly obvious. But it is still possible to configure the more serious debate within a single moral universe. There is widespread acknowledgment of a general duty to rescue others at risk, even if they are not immediate kin; there is acknowledgment of the profound dangers of policies that actively encourage the development of a homeless global proletariat, and thus an acknowledgment of the imperative to build sustainable local economies in all the world's nations; there is recognition of the irreversible cultural diversity of many developed societies and a scepticism about myths of racial and cultural purity. Once again, there are points of convergence and mutual intelligibility that can focus attention on specific questions that do not instantly appeal to ideological concerns – questions, as in our first case, of which particular policy decision risks undermining some element in the moral hinterland: when a restrictive immigration policy imposes unbearable costs on the most highly vulnerable, when a more open policy actively destabilises less developed economies by skimming off talent and enterprise,[26] and so on. If the debate is understood in this framework, it is possible to take a strong, even

---

[25] For an attempt to navigate between the poles of the debate, see Paul Collier, *Exodus. How Migration is Changing Our World*. Oxford: Oxford University Press 2013.
[26] Peter Gatrell, *The Unsettling of Europe. The Great Migration, 1945 to the Present*. London: Allen Lane 2019, chronicles in detail the ways in which migration was encouraged in the postwar period

uncompromising position on this, as on the transgender question, without assuming that only total warfare can resolve the disagreement. Tracing positions back to the 'moral hinterland' helps to weaken the tendency to focus on the immediate present of confrontation, to see present debate as symbolizing rival ideologies that are timelessly opposed; and it helps to identify specific issues of policy that might meet reasonable estimates of moral risk.

Something comparable might be discerned in the controversies over the visible legacies of slavery and colonialism, though this is still often a dialogue of the deaf.[27] Without going into detail, the irony has been noted that those uncomfortable with the demand for removing or 'contextualizing' memorials connected with slavery and racism have presented their arguments as a plea not to edit the historical record, whereas the advocates of change would (rightly) point out that the problem is an *already* edited history. Neither party, in fact, wants to suppress the past, but the serious difference is about how a more adequate moral perspective on the past is to be expressed. If statues of slavetraders are not to be removed, the memory that is conserved is effectively one that declares impartiality about their actions if there is no effort at contextual comment The question is whether the disagreement is really about edited history or is to do with the admission of historical wrongdoing (which so many societies find impossibly humiliating); both parties, in fact, assume an accountability on the part of the state and public authorities to a moral standard, and this is in itself a promising aspect to what has otherwise been a pretty sterile conflict. Once again, part of what needs doing is identifying the problem that actually needs solving on the basis of working to bring to light some shared moral concerns about truthful chronicling, and the possibility of a moral critique of one's own nation as a form of patriotism.

But to broaden the perspective and connect it with the earlier discussion, one thing that all this shows is that some of the most visible and contested markers of contemporary, self-consciously 'progressive', social conviction share more than they sometimes think with inherited moral vision: the progressivist has *learned* a perspective shared with others even when what has been learned is then put to work to extend and alter the received limits of its application. It is a point that needs reflection within the context of theological as much as political dispute. There may be disagreement about whether women can receive Holy Orders, but not about whether the Church should confer Holy Orders; there may be disagree-

---

as a deliberate strategy for the rapid rebuilding of certain European economies, focusing the question of the longer term effects of such strategies on existing inequities within and beyond Europe.

27 A relevant recent discussion in Alex von Tunzelmann, *Fallen Idols. Twelve Statues That Made History*. London: Headline 2021.

ment about the permissibility of blessing same-sex marriages, but not about the continuing significance of lifelong sexual commitment as the context both for growth in shared discipleship and for the nurture of children. The challenge is not about how the Church defends its tradition against the onslaught of contemporary theories of gender that threaten to dissolve its fundamental insights, but how the Church discerns what unavoidable new decisions will conserve a principle without destroying an 'ecology' of practice and symbol. Something of this was at least tacitly at work in the more evident discontinuities of Christian history – the acceptance of interest on loans, the abandonment of any defence of slavery, and (in practice) the radical opening-up of possibilities for women in public religious roles.

In all these instances of moral debate that are so routinely treated as a stand-off between 'tradition' and a 'revisionist' or 'feminist' or 'LGBT+' *agenda*, what we are actually seeing is a working out of Ricœur's analysis of the interaction between self-critical tradition and historically literate critique. The seductive narrative of 'culture wars', in fact, enshrines a struggle between two forms of hegemonic modernity, two sorts of ambitious ideological choice; it is heavily and destructively invested in abstract systems and so is eager to categorize this or that current problem in the terms of rival world-views competing for the allegiance of abstract individuals or groups. It directs our attention away from the actual forms of belonging across boundaries which we experience in many areas of our lives and from the shared ancestry and conceptuality of many apparently opposed views. And – as a phenomenon that exists primarily in the world of the political and religious right – it rather paradoxically adopts for itself a typically modern emancipatory rhetoric: progressivism is an unaccountable tyranny, an ideology imposed by a sacralised, mythologized system of power, repressing a minority which is denied the freedom to define itself in its own terms. As expressed in such terms, the culture wars narrative is an essentially ideological rhetoric that needs some probing and challenging, whatever position is taken on some of the contested issues. And it has to be acknowledged that there is also a rhetoric of the progressive left that gives some grounds for the reaction of 'culture warriors', a rhetoric of 'being on the side of history', being vindicated by the simple and continuous triumph of emancipatory politics as conceived by optimistic activists. The confrontation between a traditionalism determinedly in denial of its own evolution and a progressivism determinedly in denial of its contingency, and alienated from the normative and teleological assumptions of Habermasian critique (emancipation *for the sake of* proper participatory communication), is a depressing and sterile intellectual prospect.

4

Thus far, my argument has been that the ways in which we are so often encouraged to think these days about tradition and autonomy, inherited categories and innovative ideas, the nature of modernity, human solidarity and human purpose are seriously inadequate and at worst contradictory. One aspect of the work that needs doing to spring us from the trap of tribal binaries is, I suggest, a sharper attention to how arguments actually form and develop and adjust over time; so that we can see an apparently revolutionary perspective as belonging in a tradition, learned, even if obliquely, from inherited prejudgements that have survived test and scrutiny over time. It is important to do the genealogical work which allows us to see that our categories of personal dignity, our understanding of 'right' and liberty, our recognition of the claims of the vulnerable upon us do not come from nowhere; they grow from 'tradition' in the sense that they are part of a continuing argument.[28] Ultimately, what they seek to honour is what an older discourse seeks to honour; and if there is scepticism about how on earth this or that current development can indeed 'honour' what has been inherited, that scepticism needs to be spelled out in terms that can be recognized on both sides of the disagreement rather than cast in terms of an assault on what has been received or what has been immemorially agreed.

But all this is also to do with identifying more accurately what *does* need to be seen as inconsistent with the very idea of a moral tradition and thus, as a proper matter for contest. While we indulge in conventional culture warfare, we miss a conflict that is more fundamental. This is something we have touched on already in thinking about Ricœur's diagnosis of 'instrumental interest'. What he and many other since him[29] have argued is that the triumph of instrumental views means that the human subject is conceived only as the ensemble of finite and definable dispositions of wanting and choice – as it was expressed earlier, 'a sequence of problematic needs to be met or gaps to be filled.'[30] What recedes is any ground for morally serious collaboration beyond a calculation of immediate interest. If the human map is a jigsaw of territories marked out by disconnected and potentially competitive agendas for gratification, the trust that is needed for longer-term security, the trust

---

28 On this, the groundbreaking work of Larry Siedentop, *Inventing the Individual. The Origins of Western Liberalism*. London: Allen Lane 2014, is an essential point of reference.
29 In addition to Michael Sandel's work, see also the recent books of Adrian Pabst, *The Demons of Liberal Democracy*. Cambridge: Polity Press 2019, and Adrian Pabst, *Postliberal Politics. The Coming Era of Renewal*. Cambridge: Polity Press 2021.
30 Above, [7].

that comes from recognizing convergent shared concerns, has nothing to build with. So the really interesting and constructive arguments are those that turn on teasing out what in any current moral proposal can be linked to a serious trust-building tradition, and what embodies an unreflective and fragmenting instrumentalism. The point of trying to show convergent trajectories within apparently opposed attitudes to 'received' moral and cultural perspectives is that if those trajectories do indeed reflect a shared tradition that has not been fully acknowledged, if they can be located in the same overall process of learning *on the way to* participatory and just social exchange, there may be more chance of seeing clearly and critiquing effectively the implicitly anti-human ideology of instrumental interest. As Timothy Gorringe puts it:

> The constant and painful negotiation of difference does not commit us to a soggy liberalism.[31]

Testing the actual limits of difference and the extent of recognizability is not a lazy acceptance of static pluralism or an avoidance of necessary confrontation: it may be a moment in discovering where conflicts need to be brought to light – in terms not of a contest between rival, moral universes but of the contest for the very idea of a moral universe, a proper humanism as we might say, the refusal of a reductive and functionalist account of human identity.[32]

C.S. Lewis's celebrated lectures on *The Abolition of Man*, first published in 1944,[33] while commonly seen as a text to be appealed to in the canon of arguments in defence of tradition, is in fact a more ambitious project, in that it offers a prescient analysis of how 'instrumental interest' inexorably delivers human beings up to a world devoid of the possibility of emancipatory critique. The putatively objective claims made for the definition of functional success conceal the reality that a world conceived in these terms leaves no room for critique; it is bound to be a contest simply for control. It is, in that sense at least, the final triumph of 'ideology', for all the claims that may be made to transcend ideological argument. What Lewis calls

> the rule of the Conditioners over the conditioned human material, the world of post-humanity,[34]

---

31 Timothy Gorringe, *Furthering Humanity. A Theology of Culture*. London: Ashgate 2004, 258.
32 Some helpful perspectives in Jens Zimmermann (ed.), *Re-envisioning Christian Humanism. Education and the Restoration of Humanity*. Oxford: Oxford University Press 2017, especially the essays by Jens Zimmermann and Martin Schlag.
33 A new edition of the original text appeared from Harper Collins in 2021, as well as a separate volume with a very full commentary by Michael Ward, *After Humanity. A Guide to C.S. Lewis's The Abolition of Man*. New York (NY): Harper and Collins 2021.
34 C.S. Lewis, *The Abolition of Man*, 75.

is a world in which the dialogue between a tacitly moral critique (looking towards an optimal state of human participation and mutual transparency) and a complex of inherited communal moral habits and conventions of recognition or belonging will have become impossible. We do not have to share completely in Lewis's sanguine belief that a common moral culture can be read off from the facts of anthropology to see that his analysis has some common ground with Ricœur's: the problem lies with a model of human awareness and interaction that sidesteps any concern with connection or interdependence, whether between self-interrogating subjects or between the diversity of what is interrogated 'outside' subjectivity.

Tradition and critique alike are to do with the hope for, and the care and curating of, communication for the sake of common work and so of common 'culture' – that is, of a world of discourse and exchange in which people continue to know how to recognize and be recognizable to one another. The facile binaries of culture war rhetoric absolve us from the hard work of discovering whether we can in fact build a common culture at all in an age of reductive instrumentalism; but in many areas of apparent standoff it is possible to see how tradition continues to shape and mark new convictions in a way that encourages alliance and co-operation, or at least a readiness for mutual listening and learning. Not only is premature cultural despair a practically risky policy, it is also – as I have tried to show here – a strategy that can play into the hands of reductionist thinking by casting tradition as an option alongside others, an option for a certain *style* of cultural performance, in contrast to the more robust definition with which we began of cultural tradition as the entire apparatus of induction into a human world in which we must negotiate meanings we did not choose. The religious defender of tradition in this broad sense will want to articulate and to probe both the degree of unexpected convergence there may be even in the fractured moral discourses of modernity and the abiding questions raised about the transcendent ground of the moral grammar constantly and unreflectively assumed by apparently secular moral language – not least in the area of assumptions about the unique worth of the personal subject. And this means a thorough retrieval of those theologies of tradition that see it as bound up with the communal disciplines of contemplating and absorbing the vision of a human task that is ultimately about becoming fully receptive to the uncontrollable excess of divine presence and agency. In such a light, the uncontainable and irreplaceable hinterland of the finite other – that which eludes reduction to function and definition and so presents itself for unending interchange and mutual attention – is seen as a doorway into the understanding of this comprehensive task.

In such a light also, we might make sense of Ricœur's bold swerve into theology at the end of his essay on 'Hermeneutics and the Critique of Ideology', where he speculates that there would be no more interest in emancipation, no more anticipation of freedom, if the Exodus and the Resurrection were effaced from the memory of mankind...[35]

Tradition of some kinds is, as we have seen, the ground on which serious critique grows. There are 'traditional' narratives, not least, as Ricœur affirms, theological narratives, that valorize self-scrutiny, complementarity, and the significance of the time taken to clarify and transmit insight, even revealed insight. Indeed, it could be said that certain sorts of theological narrative, the kind that present the human task as one of persistent self-scrutiny in the interest of radical exposure to a truth that exceeds (even if it does not contradict) formulation, are a discipline whose absence intensifies the reductive battles of rival 'cultural' discourses. To go beyond the binaries I have been challenging, to move from 'traditionalism' to the larger question of how anything like effective cultural tradition ('tradition*ing*' as some have liked to say) can survive in our commodified social world, requires spending a bit longer with these models. What is needed is not a rush to the barricades but the attentive labour of discovering where coalitions can be built for the sake of a proper and sustained argument about moral priorities in public life – as opposed to the acceptance of an amoral instrumentalism as if it were a neutral default position, over against a tolerated set of competing options for individual consumers to construct meanings that suit them as individuals (it hardly needs saying that the educational policies of most modern states appear to have settled for this unhelpful polarity and minimized to vanishing point, the idea that education might have something to do with nourishing a capacity for morally informed critique and the imaginative enrichment this requires).[36] This, in turn, carries at least two consequences. Societies need dependable institutions of democratic participation at every level, so that learning how to argue and make decisions in the light of (often ongoing) argument becomes the common experience of citizens. And society at large needs the courage to develop large collective narratives that allow both celebration and critique of what has been received and a constantly adjusted and renewed attention to the stories of those previously silenced. Religious tradition does not exist to solve the problems of a rudderless pluralism, and its significance is not to be measured by its potential role in such a cultural environment. But it is capable of making serious contributions in the tasks just itemized, with its assumptions about continuities that are rediscovered on the far side of rupture, about the necessary complementarity of human identities and the necessary relationality of human subjectivity,

---

35 Paul Ricœur, Hermeneutics and the Critique, 100 (ellipsis in original).
36 See Jens Zimmermann (ed.), *Re-envisioning Christian Humanism*; and cf. John Haldane, *Practical Philosophy*, 260–261 on the need to allow 'comprehensive doctrines' their voice in public debate.

and about the possibility of repentance and restoration, 'realignment' with a stable metaphysical reality. Understanding the symbiotic relation between tradition and critique, between the grateful reception of inherited insight and the moral pressure to identify its failures or shortcomings, may yet deliver us from a tribalism that is as historically illiterate on the right as on the left and restore to us a sense of why it matters to resist the universal acid of functionalism and the idealising of universal systems of exchange; why it matters to keep working for the rediscovery of a symbolic order and a common social project involving the interdependent flourishing of all. Theologies and philosophies of tradition help here; the characteristically modern styles of traditionalism do not. There is harder work to be done than the slogans of the culture warrior might suggest: tradition when 'vital' – to borrow MacIntyre's word once again – has to be built not merely adopted, and that involves some fundamental work on what sort of subjects we think we are. If we do not have some sort of vocabulary for this, religious or metaphysical or whatever, we should not be surprised if we are trapped in our sealed echo chambers. To look for a sustainable anthropology is ultimately to try to do justice to the *linguistic* nature of our humanity; to the intuition that other human agents, wherever encountered, are both seriously opaque to us, to the extent that they demand we take time labouring to see and hear them more adequately, and fundamentally recognisable to us as sharing a common world.

Judith Wolfe
Reading the Signs of the Times: Theology and the Question of Progress

This conference is about change in the widest sense, but it seems to me to be particularly interested in change as progress. To what extent is progress a coherent category and a possible aim? How do we think about it practically and metaphysically, and what is the role of religions in it? These are the questions I want to focus on, speaking from my particular position as a Christian theologian, but inviting those from other standpoints – either disciplinary (religious studies) or religious (Jewish, Muslim, Eastern religions) – to contribute their perspectives in the discussion period, and of course throughout the conference. I first want to reflect on the ways 'progress' has become an intractable term to us – something that too often achieves fulfilment only at the expense of those whom it is intended to fulfil –, and then to use Christian eschatology as a tool for thinking about this intractability and about possible responses.

I want to start in *medias res*, at a time we just about remember, about 120 years ago. This was a time, when the ambition for progress in theology was tightly linked to an ideological understanding of all history as a movement of progress towards physical, moral, intellectual, and spiritual perfection. Thinkers like Hegel and Fichte saw God, described as 'Spirit' (*Geist*), as working in and through history to bring the world to the full realization of its potential: physical (through evolution and medical innovation), moral (through ever wider extension of the golden rule), intellectual (through education and research), and spiritual (through mission and nation-building). Progress was experienced as a process of self-realization of the whole world (led, of course, by Germany), which for some included that of God himself.

As early as the later 19th century, this magnificent idealist understanding of progress was widely criticized, and the catastrophes of the 20th century brought it to ruin. Most historians since Leopold von Ranke have been sceptical of the idea of progress in history: how can one tell a single, overarching developmental narrative when actors, events, and perspectives are irreducibly plural and often at odds? Within this view of history as fragmented and contingent, the question of progress in religion or theology has been unmoored from questions about progress in other fields. More than that, progress can only be understood, not to mention achieved, by identifying target goods and moving towards them. One of the most urgent questions of the 20th century has been whether it is possible to identify unified target goods that are capable of coordinating the efforts of everyone, or rather everyone that 'matters'. Over the course of the 20th and 21st centuries, we have come to see target goods as irreducibly competitive. This means that they require either intentional segregation or the violent prioritization of some goods over others. To segregate means, for example, to atomize or silo off scientific disciplines or to relativize moral frameworks and cultural customs; to prioritize violent means, for example, to impose a total regime or work towards trans-humanist goals such as the 'singularity'.

I want to look more closely at one domain in which the intractability of progress is especially acute. In scientific research and the academy, the ideal of progress is now paradigmatically associated with the natural sciences and with resulting technological advances. These advances rely on the existence of physical and chemical realities which are intelligible and manipulable. We can make progress towards the discovery, understanding, and exploitation of these entities by accumulating information and by improving methods and tools. However, it is not at all clear whether progress in that sphere is compatible or in conflict with progress towards target goods in other spheres. The potential conflict was powerfully expressed by Romano Guardini (*Letters from Lake Como*), Martin Heidegger (*The Question Concerning Technology*), C.S. Lewis (*The Abolition of Man*), J.R.R. Tolkien, and others. According to these thinkers, there is a conflict here which amounts to a crisis of the meaning of 'truth'. On the one hand, the breakdown of organisms into their component material and energy, and the exploitation of that material and energy for extrinsic ends, is in some sense 'true' to reality: it succeeds, it works. On the other hand, such atomization and exploitation are 'false' to what these organisms are: they destroy their particularity and integrity. How do we deal with this?

Pragmatically, we have dealt with it by letting the two stand side by side in the university. The university holds, or should hold, a practical balance between what we might call research and education. We, in the UK, are used to seeing research and education primarily as our two income streams. But they are something much more profound, and both are at the heart of what the university or the academy is about.

The university is a place of research. We might define research as the pursuit of truth, wherever it may lead. The university is also a place of education. Now, what is education? Education is the formation of a person who knows how to think and how to live. To believe that education is both possible and desirable requires a basic trust both in the value of the person and in the existence of a shared world in which teachers seek to orient both themselves and their students, and into which they then release their students so that they might discover and inhabit and mould that world.

Research and education are not separable from one another, because they aim at two dialectically related goods: I have elsewhere called them discovery and dwelling. On the one hand, both learning and research have to be oriented towards discovery, towards truths, regardless of their use to us. On the other hand, as long as we are human, discovery must lead back to dwelling – to living in the world with each other and ourselves. We cannot fully or ultimately abstract our knowledge from ourselves, because the truths, which we try to discover, are part of a world we have to inhabit. Learning and research always occur against the horizon of the double question: 'What kind of world are we dwelling in? – And how should we then live?'.

This lived world is not simply the world of scientific discovery; it is a set of conversations and practices, determined by questions and priorities shaped over centuries. This is why reading and knowledge have to be ever-repeated: just like faith in the Christian tradition, they have to be received and appropriated anew by each person and generation. The arts and humanities, including theology, are vital to the pursuit of knowledge not only because they discover new facts and create new data (though they sometimes do that), but because they directly address this aim of education and research, to dwell well in a world. They transmit the conversations, texts, and artefacts that have shaped our life world, and which we need to receive, engage creatively, and sometimes overcome in order to inhabit and mould it.

The sciences – particularly those employed in the service of technological innovation – discover and create possibilities in the world that sometimes outstrip our ability to live with them. This is the case now, when information technologies and (especially) interventions in what we had considered immutable nature have advanced so rapidly that we no longer find ourselves in a world we recognize. The steep rise in mental health problems in the West, despite near-unprecedented prosperity, shows that we have not yet figured out whether and how we can inhabit this new world. So, although science and technology extend the parameters within which we act, they do not answer the question of dwelling for us, but only make it urgent. The humanities can offer a vital counterweight here. But (and here is a big 'but') in reality, they often do not.

This is because we live in a world in which the ideal of education, and the idea of the human soul on which it depends, is no longer self-evidently coherent. Those of you familiar with English poetry will know the famous 19th century poem 'Dover Beach' by Matthew Arnold, an elegy to the fading of religion and a panegyric to the enduring power of poetry and of love. Hearing the long, withdrawing roar of the 'sea of faith', the poet promises to be true to his love amid the confused battles sweeping the world that has been left bare by the ebbing of religion. To the poet Matthew Arnold, and to those who followed him, the strength that endures is the sturdiness of human love, along with poetry's capacity to draw thought from nature, give form to formless anguish, and span epochs. In the universities of the late 19th and early 20th century this new humanism became the soil of a study of the Arts and Humanities untied from theological frameworks. To the sciences' rapidly advancing investigations of nature, these subjects provided a counterweighing defence of culture. But there are strong indications that in recent decades, the Humanities have experienced a crisis similar to theology's before them. To many people now, the concept of a human soul – of the human virtues, sentiments, insights, and traditions on which the humanities traditionally relied – seems as implausible and unnecessary as the concept of God. Matthew Arnold's faith in humanity is experiencing its own Dover Beach moment.

This is because the rise of technologies does not leave ideals of soul intact. The Enlightenment and its inheritors pride themselves on asserting that humans are distinguished precisely by being ends in themselves rather than fulfilling the goals of others, even God – in other words, by their particularity and integrity. Whereas nature is determined by effective causality, they argue, the will or spirit directs itself by intention. (Existentialism was, of course, a radical expression of this sense that life must be wrested from its intrinsic meaninglessness by acts of will and purpose, by achieving particularity and integrity.)

However, it is becoming increasingly clear that this second sense of human purpose, which is so fundamental to the modern West, may erode itself from within. For a long time now, we have come to suspect (as expressed so forcefully by Richard Dawkins and others) that what we regard as our own personal desires and goals are in fact genetically coded mechanisms for the perpetuation of our genetic material: mechanisms for survival and propagation which have little to do with will or personality – with particularity and integrity – as we experience them. At the same time, especially since the aggregation of 'big data', we have become more and more aware of the ways in which these desires and instincts, which guide people in choosing their 'purposes', can be conditioned and manipulated by external forces. In other words, the Western dream of humans as self-determined, free to create and choose the purposes they pursue, seems more and more like an illusion which is thrown up by our own sub-personal instincts and desires, which can in turn be manipulated by those who crack their codes and learn how to trigger our desires, fears and disgusts. Much of our economy is intended to serve the wishes of the consumer; but these wishes are themselves constantly manipulated by the system which is meant to serve them. Similarly, our political systems are in large part meant to ensure the flourishing of those whom they protect; and yet, they manipulate feelings of fear, resentment, and rivalry to dictate what counts as flourishing.

One of the dilemmas we end up with in this situation is a painful sense of contradiction between our experience of ourselves and how we seem to work in fact. We are at risk of thinking that the way we experience the world – what we regard as our own wishes, purposes, and decisions – is fundamentally illusory: that behind it all are sub-personal and super-personal forces that manipulate us like puppets on strings. This is the vision of reality played out in cultural artefacts like the Matrix films; but the films, though portraying an escape from the invisible 'matrix' of manipulation, may of course themselves be another layer of manipulation, playing on our instinctive desires for truth and freedom for the sake of box office earnings. On the one hand, this painful sense of contradiction between our experience of life and what lies behind it seems inescapable. On the other hand, it is unliveable. The acute and overwhelming mental health crisis in the Western world is in part the result not merely, as I suggested above, of technology temporarily outstripping our ability to live with it, but of a sense of life as unliveable, as fundamentally at odds with itself.

The idea of a human soul, and so of meaningful conversations across time, makes sense only if that soul is responsive to something beyond it. Humanism in itself is unstable. Lose faith in God, and you will lose faith in humans as well. We can see this as a brute anthropological datum, something that needs to be acknowledged and taken in the stride of a progress that entails overcoming the idea of the human, even at our own expense. Or we can see it as indicative of the reality of God. And is not the radical commitment to truth that is reflected in the first stance itself evidence that the mind is responsive to something beyond itself, not merely self-serving? At least part of us wants truth, even if we – the very idea of the human – must die for it.

This lecture is not the place to argue from the unliveability of a life in which deception and truth are conceptually indistinguishable to the reality of God. Instead, I want to encourage you to confront the questions raised by our situation boldly, and I want to offer a conceptual toolkit from within theology for thinking about the idea of progress within a complex environment.

This conceptual toolkit is the cluster of thought we call eschatology – the study of the last things. I have said above that the aim of education is dwelling – to live well in the world. But I have also said that such dwelling may be reliant precisely on not merely dwelling in the world: on an element not merely of homeliness but also of uncanniness. Scientific atomization may make dwelling conceptually non-sensical even when it strives to make life ever more frictionless. But philosophy and religion suggest that dwelling well is possible only against a horizon of something other or more than the mere self, or even the mere community. For Martin Heidegger, this was death itself. Humans are essentially self-reflective; and according to Heidegger, death is the condition of the possibility of that self-reflexion. This means both that we could not see ourselves if we were not mortal and that, conversely, we cannot see ourselves truly except as mortal. For the Christian tradition, too, dwelling, especially 'dwelling with God' is not a straightforward idea: it means living faithfully in the here and now, certainly; but above all, it refers to a future which is both like and radically unlike the present. In the Scriptures, to dwell with God is a promise of the end times: a promise of resurrection and of a new Jerusalem. Living well in the world depends on living in orientation towards that future: being-unto-death in Heidegger's account; living towards eternal life in the Christian.

These are eschatologies: They are accounts of life in which the question 'how should we then live?' is radically determined by the end towards which life tends – in which our identity or our history is fundamentally defined by our future. Some theologians and philosophers call this the primacy of the future. It can seem that eschatology is no longer relevant in our post-Christian age, but one of my arguments is that this is not so.

For most of Christian history, the biblical promise of Christ's Second Coming, followed by the resurrection of the dead, the Last Judgement, and the advent of the heavenly Jerusalem, guided people's understanding both of their own actions and of the times they lived in. That promise had both a moral and a historical dimension. Morally, it set all actions within the purview of an omniscient judgement to come: regardless of current inequalities and deceptions, at last the all-seeing God would weigh all deeds and judge all people equitably. Historically, it ordered all events within a divine drama leading through anguish to triumph: suffering, humiliation, and persecution were no more than the biblically foretold birth pangs of the messianic kingdom. Throughout Christian history, religious conflicts arose from disagreements of how to rightly map biblical prophecy onto the present time: whether, for example, the Pope should be understood as the vicar of Christ presiding over the thousand-year messianic reign preceding the second coming, or as the Antichrist beguiling the faithful. But these disputes did not touch the explanatory framework itself. The pressing religious question, in other words, was not how the drama of life and history was plotted, but only what role each person or group was playing in it.

The Enlightenment, challenging the reliability of revelation as a source of historical and metaphysical knowledge, inevitably changed this. After all, the last things were paradigmatically *revealed* knowledge. It was from Jesus' sayings and actions, and from biblical (and sometimes extra-biblical) prophecy, that the divine plan of salvation and judgement was known. The Enlightenment crisis of revelation was therefore, perhaps foremost, a crisis of eschatology. If Christian morality and world history were determined by their end, and the reliability of knowledge about that end was radically in question, how should one continue to talk about moral and historical action?

One of the guiding assumptions of my work (already argued in various forms by Karl Löwith, Jacob Taubes, and others) is that eschatology as a structuring frame of historical and moral thought did not become obsolescent with the Enlightenment; it was merely reworked. In other words, the standard philosophical narrative that post-Enlightenment philosophers made eschatology obsolete by formulating theories of ethics and of history that no longer depended on a divinely ordained end is too simple. Rather, eschatology was secularized in the precise sense of a transposition of the eternal into the saeculum, the age of the present world. If the crisis of revelation was a crisis of eschatology, the rise of secularization was, among other things, a transposition of eschatology: a multi-faceted endeavour to immanentize the eschaton.

There are explicit eschatologies, such as Kant's grounding of ethics in the *summum bonum* or Heidegger's being-unto-death, which deliberately anchor life in an expected end. In the political sphere, messianic promises and socially engineered utopias form the staples of political eschatologies. There are also implicit eschatologies: ways of orienting oneself in the world which are informed by expectations that remain inchoate. The story I sketched earlier, of the abolition of the concept of humanity by humanity's own scientific progress, is itself such an implicit eschatology, which can be made explicit, but affects lives whether or not it is made to do so.

In short, eschatological expectations do and always will form an indispensable part of the way we understand and experience the shape of the world and our place within it. They function as the horizons against or towards which movement is possible and makes sense. Without them, there would be no intelligible movement:

> What were we doing when we unchained this earth from its sun? Whither is it moving now? Whither are we moving? Away from all suns? Are we not plunging continually? Backward, sideward, forward, in all directions? Is there still any up or down?[1]

When the sceptics of the early 20th century rejected the large-scale, quasi-religious eschatologies of Hegel and (in some places) Marx, at least some of them thought they were bravely giving up on all coordinating systems; but that was not the case. Individuals and communities (including national communities) never lack but always hold more or less adequate eschatologies.

Some of these eschatologies are consciously catastrophic. But most are utopian in some form or other. One of the most striking things about these utopian eschatologies is that they mark deep-seated desires, but (and if I am honest, I think this is one of the basic curses of human existence) cannot help but pursue them in such ways as to destroy their objects.

Heidegger's call to being-unto-death, of course, does so intentionally. Human existence, for him, simply is to live not towards fulfilment but towards its impossi-

---

1 Friedrich Nietzsche, *The Gay Science*. Translated, with Commentary, by Walter Kaufmann. New York: Vintage Books 1974, 181.

bility. And yet for all its heroism of finitude, his tale depends for its pathos entirely on the assumption of a desire to transcend finitude which he cannot and does not attempt to account for. The passionate acts of 'shattering oneself against death' or bearing its 'affliction' which characterize authentic human existence[2] are predicated on a contrary longing which Heidegger's analysis assumes as consistently as it obfuscates it.

Historico-political eschatologies, by contrast, usually pursue collective fulfilment. Yet, they achieve it, if at all, only at the cost of redefining out of recognition either 'fulfilment' or those who obtain it. This is most obvious in those political theologies on the left and right that tend towards totalitarianism. The German Catholic convert Erik Peterson, almost unknown in English-language scholarship, was an incisive critic of such systems' failures to observe an 'eschatological reserve' (*eschatologischer Ausstand*), and his thought has not yet been exhausted as a resource for the future.[3] More complex collective eschatologies, including ascendant varieties of transhumanism, also pursue fulfilment, but acknowledge that this fulfilment is likely to bring 'the end of the world as we know it': it is not humans, but their successor AIs, who will inherit the kingdom.

This suggests that what I have described earlier as the unliveability of our technological present is in fact part of a larger pattern, which we might call the antinomy of eschatology: the irreducible tension between end as fulfilment and end as dissolution.[4] Not only in a technological utopia, but in any total aspiration, fulfilment seems to come at the expense of that which it is meant to fulfil.

This is already the case for Kant and Hegel, whose eschatologies I referenced earlier as some of the most influential modern eschatologies based not on revelation but on philosophical reasoning: in Kant's case, the changeless *summum bonum* which grounds ethics, and in Hegel's, the final state of wholeness. Kant admitted that it was a scandal to the imagination that there should be a state without change.[5]

---

[2] Cf. Martin Heidegger, *Being and Time*. Translated by John Macquarrie & Edward Robinson. Oxford: Blackwell ²1978, §§ 46–53.
[3] Erik Peterson, *Theological Tractates*. Edited and Translated by Michael J. Hollerich. Stanford: Stanford University Press 2011.
[4] See Judith Wolfe, Eschatology, in: Joel Rasmussen/Judith Wolfe/Johannes Zachhuber (ed.), *The Oxford Handbook of Nineteenth-Century Christian Thought*. Oxford: Oxford University Press 2017, 676–695, here 691; Judith Wolfe, The Eschatological Turn in German Philosophy, in: *Modern Theology 35* (2019), 55–70; here 57.
[5] Immanuel Kant, The End of All Things, in: Immanuel Kant, *Religion and Rational Theology*. Translated and Edited by Allen W. Wood, George Di Giovanni. Cambridge: Cambridge University Press 1996, 217–233; here 227.

> For a being which can become conscious of its existence and the magnitude of this existence (as duration) only in time, such a life – if it can even be called a life – appears equivalent to annihilation.[6]

And yet, the final purpose of existence, the *summum bonum*, can only be imagined as a static end, not as an infinite progress (because every stage of such a progress would be deficient by comparison to the next and therefore could not warrant contentment).[7] We cannot get away from positing this static end point, even though we also cannot imagine it without imagining it as the annihilation of life itself. Similarly, for Hegel, the identification of philosophical knowledge with *wholeness* – with

> comprehending nothing less than the entire system of consciousness, or the entire realm of the truth of spirit[8]

– is in profound tension with the philosopher's other commitment, namely to

> both knowledge and being as in their very essence dialectical and teleological processes of becoming,[9]

whose vitality lies precisely in their dynamic of growth, and for which stasis would spell death. Stanley Rosen pointedly sketches this antinomy when he writes that

> if we achieve the Hegelian science of totality, we must cease to become human.[10]

I want to spend the rest of this lecture looking more closely at Christian eschatology in relation to the fractured self of our technological present and at the antinomy of secular eschatology more generally. The expectation of the *eschata* – of resurrection, judgement and eternal life – is rooted in biblical and credal statements that the dead will rise, that Christ will judge them, and that he will gather his elect unto life everlasting. However, these claims are not *arbitrary* data of revelation, though their fanciful, sometimes even lurid, depiction throughout history can make it seem so. Rather, they define the very fabric of creation and humanity as Christi-

---

6 Immanuel Kant, The End, 227.
7 Immanuel Kant, The End, 228.
8 Georg W.F. Hegel, *Phenomenology of Spirit*. Translated by A.V. Miller. Oxford: Clarendon Press 1977, § 89.
9 Daniel Berthold-Bond, Hegel's Eschatological Vision: Does History Have a Future?, in: *History and Theory* 27 (1988), 14–29; here 16.
10 Stanley Rosen, *G.W.F. Hegel. An Introduction to the Science of Wisdom*. New Haven: Yale University Press 1974, 279; see also Alexandre Kojève, *Introduction to the Reading of Hegel*. Translated by J.H. Nichols. Ithaca (NY): Cornell University Press 1980, 158–160, n.6.

anity envisions them. In this system, creation is a gift expressing the love that *is* the trinitarian life of God. The human vocation is to be drawn, at the last, into that triune life of God: that love between Father, Son, and Spirit which defines the divine nature or life, and overflows into the creation of a non-divine world. However, this 'deification' is not a calling that is attainable by human capacities. This is because 'to be like God' does not consist (as Adam and Eve were tempted into believing in the Genesis myth) in achieving autonomy, but in being drawn (and I quote Thomas Aquinas here)

> above the condition of [our] nature to a participation of the Divine good.[11]

Therefore (and this is Aquinas again), although 'man by his nature is ordained to beatitude as his end', he is ordained to *attain* this end 'not by his own strength', but only by the 'help of grace', which draws him into the love of God.[12] This grace is poured out through the incarnation, death, and resurrection of Christ; as the Church Fathers never tire of saying, 'God became man so that man might become god'.[13] Death, once the punishment for sin, was here transformed from within into a means of sharing in the death and resurrection of Christ and so moving toward that life with God which is the innermost human calling.

This dynamic sublates the antinomy of eschatology, because it embraces both dissolution and fulfilment, and understands each through the other – Cross through resurrection, and resurrection through Cross. The New-Testament promises of the kingdom, in other words, are not simply utopian: they do not project a linear (or even a dialectical) completion of human potentiality. Instead, they require the death of the old Adam and renewed birth with Christ, 'the firstborn from the dead'.[14]

This death and re-birth with Christ mark the distinctively Christian interpretation of the claim, appearing in both the Jewish and Christian canons, that humans are 'created in the image of God'. For St Paul and St John, this means not merely that humans are like God, e.g. in being rational, but that they are united with Christ, who is the 'image of the invisible God'. Both authors describe this union in language of sight. Thus, Paul writes to the Corinthians:

> Now that Christ has been revealed, we, who with unveiled faces all reflect the Lord's glory, are being transformed into his likeness with ever-increasing glory, which comes from the Lord, who is the Spirit (2 Cor 3:18).

---

11 Thomas Aquinas, *Summa theologiae* I–II, q. 110, a. 1.
12 Thomas Aquinas, *Summa theologiae* I–II, q. 114, a. 2.
13 E.g. St. Athanasius, De incarnatione verbi 54.3.
14 Col 1:18; see also Rom 5:18, 1 Cor 15:22.

Curiously, Paul regards this not merely as a present but ultimately as an eschatological reality. The transformation he describes will not be complete until the eschaton. Thus, Paul also writes:

> Now we see in a mirror, dimly, but then we will see face to face. Now I know only in part; then I will know fully, even as I have been fully known (1 Cor 13:12).

And John echoes,

> Beloved, now are we the sons of God, and it doth not yet appear what we shall be: but we know that, when he shall appear, we shall be like him; for we shall see him as he is (1 John 3:2).

In other words, the New Testament authors imagine a future time when humans will see Christ face to face at the *parousia*; and it is then that they will also understand themselves in relationship to and reflection of him.

This is, in some ways, very far from an intuitive anthropology. Contrary to the assumption of a basic and immediate epistemological access to the self which is prerequisite to all other knowledge, here, St Paul projects knowledge (or vision) of *God* as the most direct form of self-knowledge. In the eschaton, St Paul suggests, humans will know themselves not by reflecting on themselves but by beholding God and being beheld by him. There is also an obverse side to this. If humans cannot see themselves entirely accurately in self-reflection, then this is also because the deepest wellspring of their identity is to be created, sustained, and called in love. There is no 'I' apart from that 'I' as loved by God, and there is no accurate view of that 'I' except as loved. This, too, is part of the sense of St Paul's vision:

> We now see in a mirror, dimly, but then we will see face to face. Now I know only in part; then I will know fully, even as I have been fully known (1 Cor 13:12).

This vision of humans as existentially incomplete complicates what we might say about dwelling in the world, because it bespeaks a restlessness that is not contingent but constitutive of our existence in this world. In our relationship to ourselves, this should modulate our expectations; in our relationship to others and the world, it should modulate our attachments. But the theological account is carefully calibrated: The human desire for completion is one that neither rests content within the world nor stands over against it: all human relationships of love anticipate it, and all care for the world prepares for it.

I began by reflecting on the 19th century ideal of overarching progress and on the fracturing of that ideal by the early 20th century. I talked about the experience of an irreducible tension between competing ideals, which made the very notion of progress problematic, partial, or potentially violent. I focused more closely on the competing ideals of human dwelling in the world on the one hand and atomization for the sake of discovery and mastery on the other, and I talked about their unstable coexistence in the contemporary university. I then argued that the tension between these ideals was in some ways not particular to our own time but part and parcel of what I called the antinomy of eschatology, namely that goal towards which a system strives to is often at once its fulfilment and its dissolution – or, to put it differently, that it is very hard to pursue something in such a way that it will not destroy either the object or the seeker. I then reflected theologically on Christian eschatology, which in one particular way makes sense of this antinomy and presents a vision of human identity as resting not in oneself but in reflecting and responding to God.

I have spoken as a theologian rather than a scientist of religion, and my arguments have been philosophical and theological ones. It is a separate question whether and how such arguments can be made fruitful within the study of religion, but I encourage us to try. More generally, in this Academy, both approaches to religion – theology and religious studies or science of religion – are strongly represented, and I hope very much that we can learn from one another without immediately seeing each other either as unserious or as threats. This is difficult, because the driving assumptions of the two fields can be directly opposed. Religious studies or the scientific study of religion tends to begin from the assumption that explanation must be ultimately naturalistic: human behaviour follows patterns that are explicable in naturalistic terms and generalizable across domains. Religious experience is therefore analyzable as a variety of hyperactive agency detection or as a resolution of mental prediction error that over-prioritizes schematic priors over sense data; religious institutions are social hierarchies whose roles and dogmas are prestige carriers that can be analyzed functionally without remainder. Christian theology, by contrast, as I have shown, tends to begin from the assumption that belief can transform people at the deepest level because it reveals a world that transcends the structures that are basic to the naturalistic conception of human psyche and society: above all, the conditions of scarcity that animate evolutionary and social dynamics. Theology's basic claim is that, on some level, the world is or can be radically different than it appears through a naturalistic lens. It is a matter of theological debate where that level is primarily located: in the individual, in communities, in the past, or hoped-for future. It is also a matter of debate what the exact nature of this radical difference is. I have given a brief picture of the difference as seen through the lens of Christian eschatology.

In this situation of polarity, it is important not to insist on premature closure from either side. Real dynamism can come from remaining open to each other. Religious studies scholars remind theologians not to turn a blind eye to the common psychological and social dynamics operating in religious people and communities. If the cognitive processes at work in charismatic prayer resemble those at work in certain types of aesthetic experience, or if the social hierarchies of religious orders display the same risks and failure modes as those of insular societies, theologians cannot ignore these insights. Conversely, theologians like me ask scientists of religion to be methodologically agnostic rather than naturalistic. Even if religious scientists are sceptical of the metaphysical claims made by theologians, their encounter with these alternative explanatory frameworks may yet spur new discoveries. The difficult problem of consciousness, for instance, may not be solvable on current scientific paradigms, and theology is one of the domains generating alternative hypotheses.

In closing, therefore, I want to advocate a more modest vision of progress, which trusts in the dynamic force of theology and of dialogue. Dynamic, from Greek *dynamis*, strength, means both 'force producing motion' and 'force in action'. Theology should be both force producing motion and force in action. It should be generative of new light and change in other disciplines (producing motion) and also take into itself the discoveries of other disciplines (in action). We can build on many examples of theology as a force producing motion, both historical and current. In science, the comprehensibility of the cosmos that is assumed by a theistic account of creation propelled 'natural philosophy', i.e. scientific enquiry; in society, the New-Testament-ideals of equality and mercy created radically new social and political systems, which are still developing; in psychology, the Trinitarian view of God as three persons in essential relation propelled views of personhood that have defined our civilization. Such theological impulses are not only historical, but also current: In philosophy, the experience of transcendence encourages new research into how we encounter reality (both in analytic and in continental thought); in political theory, eschatology is catalyzing new theories about history. There are also, of course, many examples of theology as a force in action, affected by other domains. Historically, study of other cultures and religions has forced theologians to think in more differentiated ways about groups which they had been happy to generalize about earlier, and thus effectively to exclude from their theologizing. Ongoingly, evolution is making us think very seriously about equations of natural fact with divine will.

In this sense, the place of theology and religion in the university can also be that of a tentpole: a field that both enables and seeks open-ended conversations with other subject areas, because of a conviction that we inhabit a shared world, and that that world admits of investigation. This also means that theology is (not necessarily in every instance, but in basic orientation) interdisciplinary. Because theology relates people and fields to each other, it must be responsive to their questions, discoveries, and challenges. If theology seeks to understand not just one narrow subject matter but a shared whole, then, it is only as good as its understanding of the world which it seeks to illuminate. And such understanding can only be achieved by open, critical, and constructive conversation with people from different backgrounds. This is an endeavour that counts as 'progress' on many different maps of meaning, and I encourage us all to pursue it together in these days.

Vassilis Saroglou
Sameness, Adaptation, or Change? Understanding the Specifics and Limits of Religious Change

1

Asking the question of whether religion as an institution, and religiousness as a personal disposition regarding a specific domain of life, change or remain the same over time, may, at first glance, appear a very trivial question. Institutions, living entities, and individuals both change, to some extent, and remain the same, again, to some extent. We perceive and understand things and people as having some essence and identity and at the same time, as also evolving under the influence of time as they exist in constantly changing living environments.

However, the question above, regarding religious change is much more complex and, to my knowledge, has not yet been examined from a psychological perspective.[1] Besides the trivial idea that religion both changes and remains the same, a series of fascinating questions arises. Is religious continuity – and thus sameness – more important and powerful in individuals and groups than religious change, or is it the opposite? Moreover, is continuity in institutional religion and individual religiousness quantitively more or less substantial than continuity in other similar, traditional and historical, institutions and other proximal individual dispositions such as personality traits, social attitudes, and values? Alternatively, it may be that religion is characterized by specific ways through which change and continuity are operationalized. Thus, the difference between religion and other domains of human activity that appear more evolutive, such as politics, economy, or leisure, may be rather qualitative. Furthermore, what are the psychological mechanisms that could explain religious continuity/sameness and religious change? Finally, what are the psychological mechanisms that may be particularly relevant and thus, theologically interesting for understanding the resistance to change in religion?

In this work, I will present an initial examination of the questions above. From a psychological perspective, the emphasis will be on people's religiousness and reli-

---

[1] See, for a recent exception, Joshua C. Jackson et al., The New Science of Religious Change, in: American Psychologist 76 (6/2021), 838–850, an article published concomitantly to the 2021 conference of the European Academy of Religion where the present work was presented as a keynote lecture.

Open Access. © 2023 Vassilis Saroglou, published by De Gruyter. This work is licensed under the Creative Commons Attribution 4.0 International License.
https://doi.org/10.1515/9783111241463-004

gious experience, i.e., their ideas, affects, values, and behavior in relation to their religion. I will thus focus much less or not at all on religion as an institution implying normative beliefs, rituals, norms, and community, the continuity or change of which belongs, of course, to the expertise of theologians and historians. The present work may be of interest for psychologists of religion who are sometimes too focused on the research literature of their generation and/or the very specifics of their own context to engage in broader consideration of research across decades, potentially missing the 'big picture'. It may also be of interest for theologians and religious scholars who, depending on their personal preferences, could overemphasize either continuity or change when considering religion from a macro perspective.[2]

2 Religious Continuity and Change

Religion and religiousness both change and remain the same. Nevertheless, the two processes may not operate equally. They may each be colored by specific features compared to other domains of human activity. Furthermore, there seems to be notable discrepancies between the dynamics for change and the pressure for continuity. I will examine these issues here mostly through a series of examples.

2.1 Strong Religious Continuity, Sameness, and Inertia

By their very nature, religions are institutions whose authority comes from a foundational past and whose expertise is guaranteed only to the degree that some continuity exists with what is perceived to have been fundamental (text, credo, ritual, ministry). Not surprisingly thus, religions are heavily influenced by dynamics favoring maintenance, sameness, and inertia. Similarly, religionists, to be perceived by themselves and others as members of the community, need to believe, feel, and/or behave, if only to a minimal degree, in accordance with what is consid-

---

[2] Note that I focus on this work, from a social psychological perspective, on religious continuity and change across time and not on religious changes as a function of age and human development. For the latter, see Vassilis Saroglou, *The Psychology of Religion*. London/New York: Routledge 2021, chapter 3: Theist Children, Apostate Adolescents, Bigot Late Adults? and Paul Wink/Michele Dillon/Dan Farina, Religion, Spirituality, and the Agential Self, in: Dan P. McAdams/Rebecca L. Shiner/Jennifer L. Tacket (eds.), *Handbook of Personality Development*. New York: Guilford 2019, 364–379, for recent reviews.

ered as normative.[3] The non-respect, even minimal, of such conformity with some of the features considered to be fundamental to the religion constitutes a reason for exclusion, be it by oneself, by others, or by the community.

For these reasons, it may be tempting to characterize religion as one of the domains of human cultural activity with the greatest degree of continuity, sameness, and inertia. Quantitatively speaking, compared to religion, other domains such as politics, economy, work, education, art, leisure, and even law, with its high internal coherence, and kinship systems, heavily based on biology, are characterized by greater transformative dynamics and higher flexibility regarding what constitutes authority and what defines expertise.

Undoubtedly, the observer, familiar with contemporary Western Protestantism and Catholicism, is aware of important recent developments and changes within these denominations. These developments have certainly had an impact even on aspects of religion that are typically highly resistant to change, such as rituals and the Church's organization. Very likely, the strong pressure from modern values of individual autonomy and societal secularism has facilitated such developments. Nevertheless, these developments within Western Christianity seem to be the exception when one considers the larger worldwide religious landscape.

For instance, in Orthodox Christianity, a denomination with which I am, for family reasons, quite familiar, religionists continuously oppose even the smallest superficial and cosmetic changes in very secondary aspects of faith and practice. They do so even in opposition to their religious authorities – bishops, Patriarchs, Synods – who occasionally try to introduce such changes to better serve their pastoral mission and the believers' spiritual needs. To give one simple example, these religionists still oppose the replacement of the Byzantine Greek or Slavonic texts and hymns of religious services, which nobody fully understands anymore, with modern language. The recent Covid-19 pandemic revealed that religious conservatives within Orthodox Christianity are, across countries, an important part of the community. These religionists have succeeded in opposing even the simplest changes in order to avoid contamination, such as the use of distinct individual tongs instead of a communal one for the reception of the Holy Communion.

Indeed, what appears in Western Christianity to be the expression of only a minority's religious conservatism, orthodoxy, or fundamentalism, constitutes a substantial part of everyday religious life in many other religions and denominations. Thus, we must be cautious not to conclude that religion, with the exception of conservative and fundamentalist tendencies, undergoes significant global changes. This is not to say that some religions are necessarily more conservative

---

[3] Jean-Pierre Deconchy, *Orthodoxie religieuse et sciences humaines*. The Hague: Mouton 1980.

or fundamentalist than others: such a qualification must take the cultural context into account. It suggests though that religious continuity, sameness, and inertia are much more important that some may think.

2.2 Highly Discrete Religious Developments and Changes

At the same time, changes are also undergone in religion and religiousness. These changes sometimes occur in a blatant, explicit, and rapid way; take, for instance, the process and outcomes of the Vatican II Council. Most often, however, changes are more progressive, implicit, and slow. Similarly, religious developments that appear to be significant changes are actually not as radical or accomplished as one could imagine. I will present a few examples that refer specifically to how religiousness and related spirituality and ethics may change, but also how these changes are more modest than believed – with the discrepancy often being between theological developments and people's everyday religiousness.

Humor was considered with suspicion in the Patristic era. Laughter, at least 'immoderate' laughter, was perceived as indicating that a person had lost self-mastery. It was thus condemned in Middle Age Christian spirituality. Today, theological essays tend to rehabilitate humor and laughter by finding humorous elements in the Bible, or at least by re-interpreting some biblical passages as potentially intended to be humorous. Christian, ethical, and spiritual essays tend to praise humor and laughter as a human expression that allows for self-transcendence. Nevertheless, empirical psychological research shows that even in the 2000s and the 2010s, and even in Western secularized societies, individual religiousness, and not only fundamentalism, is still accompanied by some discomfort in creating, using, and appreciating humor in general or at least many types of humor.[4]

Sexuality, not only extra-marital or pre-marital, but also sexuality within marriage, has traditionally been considered as morally and spiritually suspicious or potentially dangerous, and this has been true across all major religious traditions. Recent theological developments have contributed to a more positive reconsideration of body, senses, emotions, and sexuality, at least sexuality within heterosexual married couples, as being valuable and as potentially facilitating religious and spiritual life. Nevertheless, there is substantial recent evidence across cultures and

---

[4] Vassilis Saroglou, Religion and Sense of Humor. An A Priori Incompatibility? Theoretical Considerations from a Psychological Perspective, in: *Humor: International Journal of Humor Research 15* (2/2002), 191–214 and Vassilis Saroglou, Religion, in: Salvatore Attardo (ed.), *Encyclopedia of Humor Studies. Volume 2.* Thousand Oaks (CA): Sage 2014, 636–641 for reviews.

religions showing the persistence of the religion-sexuality conflict. This conflict is present even among young people and adults living today in secularized Christian Western contexts. As this research shows, religiousness, i.e., being a believer or a strong believer compared to being a non-believer, is to some extent accompanied by less frequent sexual behavior, even among married couples, but also by lower sexual desire and higher sexual guilt – not to mention the clearly negative attitudes toward unconventional sexuality.[5]

Another area of interest where one can observe religious change on the basis of psychological empirical evidence is that regarding intergroup relations and outgroup prejudice and discrimination – a universal human phenomenon resulting from group belonging and collective identity. A variety of outgroups exists for religionists: religious (members of other religions or denominations), ideological (e.g., atheists), ethnic/racial, and moral (e.g., gay people, single mothers). Contrary to what we could expect based on the spiritual values of tolerance and compassion, research has rather consistently shown that religious people, not only fundamentalists, but also mere believers and practitioners, tend to have not only negative attitudes toward several kinds of outgroups, but also to express these attitudes through discriminatory behavior and, in some cases, through behavioral hostility. However, a closer examination of the empirical research on religious prejudice in the last 50–60 years shows two interesting dynamics attesting to both continuity and change. On the one hand, prejudice as a function of individual religiousness is rather constant across decades with regard to moral outgroups, in particular homosexuals, and ideological outgroups, in particular atheists.[6] On the other hand, change has been observed regarding ethnic/racial outgroups. When racism became socially explicitly proscribed, religiousness was no longer, or at least much less frequently, found to predict ethnic and racial prejudice.[7] Going further, some studies have suggested that, at least in Western Europe, intrinsic religiousness may

---

5 Vassilis Saroglou, Religion and Related Morality Across Cultures, in: David Matsumoto/Hyisung C. Hwang (eds.), *The Handbook of Culture and Psychology*. New York: Oxford University Press ²2019, 724–785 for review.
6 Wade C. Rowatt/Tom Carpenter/Megan Haggard, Religion, Prejudice, and Intergroup Relations, in: Vassilis Saroglou (ed.), *Religion, Personality, and Social Behavior*. New York: Psychology Press 2014, 170–192 and Vassilis Saroglou, Intergroup Conflict, Religious Fundamentalism, and Culture, in: *Journal of Cross-Cultural Psychology* 47 (1/2016), 33–41 for reviews.
7 C. Daniel Batson/Patricia Schoenrade/W. Larry Ventis, *Religion and the Individual. A Social-psychological Perspective*. New York: Oxford University Press 1993 and Deborah Hall/David Matz/Wendy Wood, Why Don't We Practice What We Preach? A Meta-Analytic Review of Religious Racism, in: *Personality and Social Psychology Review* 14 (1/2010), 126–139.

also predict tolerance of ethnic groups and immigrants and valorization of multiculturalism.[8]

The examples above of modest but observable changes are all in the progressive direction, i.e., promoting the so-called self-expressive and emancipative values. Importantly, though, there are examples of changes that seem to go in the opposite direction, i.e., increased conservatism and withdrawal to one's own community. I do not refer to phenomena here where a specific community becomes radicalized – see, for instance, the developments in some components of American Evangelicalism, occurring at the same time as other Christian denominations in the US were becoming more liberal. But here, rather, I refer to the way religion, or more precisely religious culture in society as a whole, becomes more conservative. For instance, in the Christian Orthodox world, for many decades of the 20th century, the adjective 'Christian' was broadly used to qualify all kinds of religious elements: for instance, Christian baptism, Christian faith, Christian art, and Christian spirituality. However, starting in the eighties, the adjective 'Christian' has progressively been almost fully replaced by the adjective 'Orthodox'. Lay people, practitioners, theologians, and religious authorities typically speak of Orthodox spirituality, Orthodox baptism and marriage, Orthodox faith, or Orthodox ethics.[9]

2.3 The Developments-Continuity Discrepancy: An Issue of Temporal Delay or of Overestimation of Change?

Several examples we presented in the previous sections suggest that religious continuity, not to say sameness, is in fact stronger, from a macro perspective, than it may appear to those very familiar with religion, who often apply a micro perspective in their understanding. Theological and intra-religious developments are in principle complex, nuanced, rich, and evolutive. However, when one focuses on what religiousness implies in people's life, in terms of related cognition, affects, values, and behavior, it is the persistence of many religious features that predominates change. On the basis of the examples we described, this persistence may include, among

---

[8] Stefanie Doebler, Relationships Between Religion and Intolerance Towards Muslims and Immigrants in Europe: A Multilevel Analysis, in: *Review of Religious Research 56* (1/2014), 61–86 and Tufan Ekici/Deniz Yucel, What Determines Religious and Racial Prejudice in Europe? The Effects of Religiosity and Trust, in: *Social Indicators Research 122* (1/2015), 105–133.

[9] Importantly, this need to accentuate distinctiveness and uniqueness in the context of globalization, especially with respect to the West and Western Christianity, can be put in parallel with tendencies within contemporary Islam to accentuate its uniqueness with regard to a supposedly decadent West and Europe.

many other aspects, (a) beliefs, such as magical thinking regarding the efficiency of ritual, (b) ethics, such as restrictive attitudes toward sexuality, (c) intergroup attitudes, such as prejudice against convictional and moral outgroups, and (d) belonging to a tradition and community perceived as unique and superior to other ones.

One way to interpret the discrepancy above is to argue that there is often a delay between developments 'in theory' and changes 'in practice'. Specifically, there may be a discrepancy between theological and official ecclesiastic discourse, which may rapidly evolve, on the one hand and what religious people really do in their everyday lives on the other hand. The latter is more easily marked by inertia, faithfulness to tradition, and continuity with early religious socialization. This explanation in terms of 'delay' is certainly valid in several cases but becomes difficult to accept when we observe delays for decades or centuries.

An alternative, possibly complementary, explanation is that theologians and religious leaders overestimate the presence and salience of religious change. They insert these changes in their representations but may be unaware of the empirical reality of believers' lives being marked more strongly by continuity. Alternatively, they may defensively pretend that important changes have been made, though in fact these changes are extremely subtle – even at the explicit discourse level.

A salient example that nicely illustrates the above is the concurrence of very timid developments and strong continuity regarding religious homophobia. Empirical research in the psychological and social sciences of religion in the last 50–60 years has consistently shown that mere religiousness, not only fundamentalism, is typically associated, across various cultural and religious contexts, with not only the de-consideration of homosexuality as being both morally and socially problematic, but also with prejudice and the behavioral discrimination of homosexual people.[10] Theological developments, at least in Western Christianity in the last decades, have advanced more liberal interpretations of biblical texts which were traditionally considered as condemning homosexuality. Moreover, recently, in mainstream Protestantism and Catholicism, there have been considerable developments in principle. Notably, a distinction is made today between (a) homosexual orientation, considered as given by nature and thus not being subject to moral judgment, and (b) the sexual behavior of gay people, condemned as immoral. In addition, several religions insist today on the importance of distinguishing between (a) condemning the sin (homosexuality) and (b) loving the sinner (the gay person).

Have these developments been translated into empirical reality, in terms of what religionists think, feel, and do? Yes and no. Overall, among believers in the West, there has been an attenuation of sexual prejudice, following the broader

---

[10] Vassilis Saroglou, Religion and Related Morality, 724–785 for review.

tendencies of secular societies. However, surprisingly enough, empirical research using subtler methods (experimental designs, behavioral measures) attests of the continuous prevalence of religious prejudice and even the behavioral discrimination of gay people.[11] Indeed, the same religionists who, in principle, explicitly endorse the sin-sinner distinction are unable to apply this distinction when their behavior is tested in the lab. For instance, they will be less willing to help a gay person even to accomplish noble goals like visiting a grandmother or finding a job if unemployed.[12] Going further, an international study showed that the endorsement of the belief in the sin-sinner distinction serves to legitimize sexual prejudice.[13]

3 How Religion and Religiousness Change

There are various kinds and modalities of change. To the measure that religious changes occur, one may wonder what the specific modalities of these changes within the religious sphere are and what the implications of these modalities are. Furthermore, one may wonder whether these changes have a particular direction or whether all directions are (equally) possible. A question related to this is whether the direction of religious change parallels the direction of broader societal changes or not. Below are some tentative answers to these questions.

3.1 Religious Change as (Only) Adaptation

The clear predominance of religious continuity over change is mainly due to what we mentioned in the introduction of this work: religion's very nature and authenticity, particularly in the believer's eyes, strictly depends on its capacity to demonstrate some sort of fidelity to the original fundamental truth. This truth may be initiated by a founder figure, described in a sacralized text, or simply experienced by previous generations.

---

[11] Vassilis Saroglou, Religion and Related Morality, 724–785 for review.
[12] C. Daniel Batson et al., 'And Who Is My Neighbor?:' Intrinsic Religion as a Source of Universal Compassion, in: *Journal for the Scientific Study of Religion 38* (4/1999), 445–457 and Lynne M. Jackson/Victoria M. Esses, Of Scripture and Ascription: The Relation Between Religious Fundamentalism and Intergroup Helping, in: *Personality and Social Psychology Bulletin 23* (8/1997), 893–906.
[13] Mark Romeo Hoffarth/Gordon Hodson/Danielle S. Molnar, When and Why Is Religious Attendance Associated With Antigay Bias and Gay Rights Opposition? A Justification-Suppression Model Approach, in: *Journal of Personality and Social Psychology 115* (3/2018), 526–563.

This constraint also influences the way change is operationalized within religion. It implies that when religious change is initiated, discussed, and implemented, it must be presented mainly as only an adaptation of the same original truth and its acculturation with regard to a changing societal environment and a new cultural context. This implies some, or even an important, re-interpretation of the original truth but certainly in a way that demonstrates continuity if not sameness with that truth. As a consequence, the change, while well-proclaimed, may be superficial and less important than it is perceived to be; or on the contrary, change may be significant even if it is presented as only a slight adaptation. In other words, in religion, sameness often prevails despite claims of change, but changes occur beyond the rhetoric of continuity and mere adaptations.

3.2 Sameness Even if Claiming Change

The above features constitute a critical specificity of religion with regard to many other domains of cultural human activity. For instance, in politics, science, art, economy, education, and even law, to cite a few interesting examples, changes are proposed, discussed, and implemented most often on the basis of a cost-benefit rationale – which of course may include the adaptation rhetoric, among other things. But there is not necessarily a need to demonstrate or pretend to demonstrate continuity or fidelity with a previously endorsed truth or value. Of course, institutions and organized groups use the argument of fidelity to their fundamental values and principles, or their constitution, but this discourse is usually complemented by cost-benefit rationales. More importantly, non-religious institutions and groups can change and rewrite the chart of their fundamental values, principles, and constitution.

Religious change as adaptation is thus a very specific type of change. For the purpose of this work, I typed the world 'change' into Google Images and observed the diversity with which change is depicted across the many images that appeared. This led to a nice typology of the various representations of change. Change may be represented – and is thus perceived – as a slight or a radical shift of direction, as partial or full replacement, as a timely necessity, as an entire transformation, as an optimistic transition from impossibility to possibility, as progress and advance ahead, as the product of a discursive process, and/or as a reagencement of pre-existing pieces with some creation of new space. Based on what I have developed in this work, religious change most often adheres to the model of change as an adaptation to time and less frequently, not at all, or only occasionally to the other models of change.

An implication of religious change experienced mainly as adaptation is the implicit assumption that time and the changes time introduces denote the mutability and thus imperfection of human nature and human affairs. Only God is immutable and remains the same, since only God is perfect – or alternatively, thus only God is perfect. This model of religious change as a necessary adaptation to societal changes emphasizes an essentialist perception of truth as pre-existing and already established rather than as an objective for the future or a reality that is progressively built. Subsequently, significant large-scale changes are suspected of making substantial alterations of this pre-existing truth.

3.3 Change Under the Guise of Continuity

A way to implement religious change while still maintaining or pretending to maintain continuity and even sameness is to distinguish between primary and central versus secondary and peripheral aspects of the truth or norm that is about to be changed. Primary elements should be preserved, secondary elements can be changed. Similarly, to implement religious changes, one needs to preserve the spirit of the original text or norm by proposing a so-called symbolic instead of literal interpretation. Whereas there is usually a certain consensus among scholars, religionists, and religious leaders regarding the principle of the above conceptual distinction, typically, there is much less consensus on which specific features can be considered secondary and which elements should be preserved as primary. Similarly, there is criticism as to whether a particular symbolic interpretation may go too far and violate the spirit of the original belief, norm, or practice.

More importantly, the distinction between secondary and primary religious elements, or between a symbolic and a literal interpretation, is never established a priori. It must be negotiated and is subject to future developments. An interpretation perceived as symbolic today in a given religious community (e.g., 'Christians will have a new life in eternity with God'; instead of 'Christians, with a new body, will be resurrected at some point in the future') may end up being perceived as a literal interpretation of the belief in resurrection decades and generations later and be replaced by a new, more symbolic and abstract interpretation such as 'life is stronger than death'.

This process of continuously redefining across centuries what is, and will remain, primary and central while other elements which were previously considered to be primary undergo a process of reconsideration as secondary, allows for the implementation of significant changes under the guise that continuity has prevailed and that the change was only an adaptation. For instance, contemporary Protestants' religious lives differ notably from believers' lives in the early years of

Christianity, despite the fact that the many changes that have occurred since then were most often experienced as mere adaptations or as a rediscovery, in a new context, of the original truth.

3.4 Direction of Religious Change: Liberalization or Rigidification and Polarization?

The direction(s) of religious change throughout history constitutes an interesting matter. This topic is typically addressed by historians, but psychologists, together with other social and behavioral scientists, can examine the direction of religious changes in recent decades, and in particular in the context of increasingly secularized societies, on the basis of modern empirical data. Two scenarios appear intellectually meaningful.

First, religion and religiousness may align with more general cultural and societal changes. Thus, one can expect self-expressive and emancipative values, which have been found to go hand in hand with secularism, to exert their pressure. Religiousness should thus become more autonomous, more individualized, less traditional, and be less characterized by collectivistic values of loyalty to the ingroup and respect for authority.[14] Note that there is cross-cultural evidence that societies in general, and not only Western ones, are becoming less collectivistic and are emphasizing autonomy and individuality to an increasing degree.[15] As a consequence, faith and religious practice in secularized societies are likely to be more an issue of personal choice than of family education and societal socialization. Similarly, belief and practice are more likely to be intrinsically, rather than extrinsically, motivated: they are based on motivations directly related to faith and spiritual objectives rather than external interests and goals.

Second, it may be that religiousness, in the context of secularism, is prone to defensiveness, thus becoming more rigorous, conservative, and absolutist in beliefs, practice, norms, and group identity. Becoming a minority gradually, religionists may be tempted to radicalize, at least if we adopt the optimal distinctiveness theory.[16] This theory implies, among others, that minority groups feel the need

---

14 Pippa Norris/Ronald Inglehart, *Sacred and Secular. Religion and Politics Worldwide*. New York: Cambridge University Press ²2012.
15 Henri C. Santos/Michael E.W. Varnum/Igor Grossmann, Global Increases in Individualism, in: *Psychological Science 28* (9/2017), 1228–1239.
16 Geoffrey J. Leonardelli/Cynthia L. Pickett/Marilynn B. Brewer, Optimal Distinctiveness Theory: A Framework for Social Identity, Social Cognition, and Intergroup Relations, in: *Advances in Experimental Social Psychology 43* (2010), 63–113.

to accentuate their differences from the majority to preserve their own visibility and identity. As a consequence, such rigidification should imply increasing polarization in secular societies between strong religionists on the one hand, and strong atheists and secularists on the other hand.[17]

Extensive research from the social and behavioral sciences, having focused on various questions relevant to the above issue, has provided convergent results.[18] Rigidification followed by polarization is not to be excluded but constitutes, quantitatively speaking, only a minor phenomenon. It often applies to minority religious groups under tension and experiencing discrimination for ethnoreligious reasons. But it is the first scenario that looks predominant, with religiousness overall following, to some extent, the liberalization and individualization of values and worldviews in secularized societies. In parallel, compared to the past, religiousness is changing, becoming more intrinsic, more spiritual, more prosocial, and more tolerant of various kinds of outgroups.

Nevertheless, an impression of some polarization still exists, in terms of a stronger contrast, compared to the past, between nonbelievers and religious believers, on several moral issues for instance. Interestingly, recent sociological research has demonstrated that the impression of polarization we may have is not due to religious believers becoming more conservative and reactive – if anything, they have become more liberal – but rather to atheists and secularists whose stance has shifted more significantly as they have become increasingly liberal. In traditional religious societies, there is simply more consensus regarding many moral issues and worldviews.

4 Sources of Religious Change

Even under the strong pressure for continuity, if not sameness, and even if often limited in scope, religious changes do occur regularly. What are the sources of such changes? It is reasonable to assume that both (a) factors external to religion, societal and cultural ones, and (b) factors internal to religious life and experience exert their influence, independently or jointly, in generating religious changes.

---

[17] Egbert Ribberink/Peter Achterberg/Dick Houtman, Religious Polarization: Contesting Religion in Secularized Western European Countries, in: *Journal of Contemporary Religion* 33 (2/2018), 209–227.
[18] Vassilis Saroglou, Religion and Related Morality, 724–785.

4.1 External Sources

All kinds of societal and cultural developments are of course important external sources of religious change. Obviously, as evoked above, secularization in the recent decades has been a major source of religious changes. Additionally, political developments, democratization, law transformations, economic crises, sociological changes, geographical mobility, demographic changes, changes in the relationships between Churches and the State, moral liberalization, scientific advances – including the development of sciences of religion, intergroup conflicts, wars, diseases, and natural disasters have been found to influence not only the mean level of religiousness and secularism in societies but also the nature of people's religiousness and the way it is expressed.

For instance, scientific advances in the understanding of the origins of homosexuality have helped major religions to reconsider, to some extent, their attitudes toward persons of sexual minorities. The legalization of issues like abortion and euthanasia has pushed many religious Westerners to tolerate the fact that others have the right to behave differently and to not embrace such religious moral prohibitions. Immigration, multiculturalism, and globalization have contributed to the decrease of religious exclusivism and to the increase of interreligious understanding and tolerance. Urbanization has decreased the social pressure in rural environments to practice religion and to be a regular part of the community. Societies with less disease, deaths, and health problems have been found to also be societies where religiousness is less salient on average and does not necessarily have an additional contributing role with regard to well-being – as do many other societal sources.

Thus, most often, religious changes are provoked or encouraged by these external sources of pressure. Religions aim to accommodate themselves to these developments. Otherwise, as history and sociology of religion have emphasized, major religions and communities take the risk of becoming marginal minorities or even being extinguished. (On the contrary, if they become too similar to the environing society, they end up being non-attractive).

4.2 Internal Sources

Nevertheless, there are also internal sources of change within religion. First, theological and ecclesiastic developments by themselves may generate or enable changes – for good or bad. In the Catholic world, Vatican II has been a golden example and its transformative influence has been long-lasting. In the Christian Orthodox world, the late 20th century rediscovery of Patristic theology and ancient monastic spirituality, in combination with the opening of postgraduate programs in the departments of Orthodox theology (which reduced the departure of young Orthodox theologians in the West) contributed, together with external causes, to the phenomenon of orthodoxism, i.e., no longer self-identifying as Christian, but exclusively as Orthodox.

Second, religious changes occur due to the influence of the so-called prophetic voices and charismatic figures within religious communities, as well as the originality and attractiveness of the message and action of religious figures who have been foundational to a specific religious movement or even a new religion.

Typically, within religious communities, individuals who dispose of the power of charisma (i.e., are admired for their exemplary and authentic spirituality and their prototypicality in incarnating the group's values) are influential and initiate, orient, or circumscribe changes. Their power for change is most often more important than the influence of other persons with power of legitimacy (high rank ministers) or mere expertise (theologians).

In addition, founders of religious movements and new religions are, almost by definition, initiators of more radical changes; most often they instigate change by criticizing the limitations and even the inauthenticity of the religious expressions of a given environment. Founders of new religions and initiators of religious movements and successful schisms are great actors of changes in the world's religious landscape. They do so either by proposing a new, more authentic and faithful, interpretation of the original message of a given religion, or by creating the basis for a new religion and implicitly or explicitly signaling the limitations of the other religions.

4.3 Conservatives and Liberals: Stable Interindividual Differences

Finally, religious changes or religious continuity and sameness can simply be explained by the fact that religionists, including religious authorities, as humans in general, are characterized by important interindividual variability. A key personality dimension on which people within the same society and the same group show important variability with each other is high versus low openness to experience.[19] This personality dimension denotes high or low propensity for novelty, variety, and complexity, instead of routine, sameness, and simplicity, and does so across all

---

[19] Robert R. McCrae/Angelina R. Sutin, Openness to Experience, in: Mark R. Leary/Rick H. Hoyle (eds.), *Handbook of Individual Differences in Social Behavior*. New York: Guilford 2009, 257–273.

domains of life and human activity. It thus includes high versus low open-mindedness regarding ideas, values, and worldviews, and high versus low flexibility and openness to change regarding practices and behavior.

It is of importance to note that this interindividual variability is partly determined by genetic and biological dispositions. Subsequently, non-negligible long-term stability exists, for years, or even decades, in being high, low, or simply on average on this personality dimension – as for many other individual differences.[20] A practical implication of this is that people who are religious conservatives or religious liberals will very likely continue to be so for years, if not decades. If they change, their change on this dimension – as for other personality dimensions – will not be radical but rather modest in size. This accentuates the impression we have of the distance between the two positions, the religious conservatives and the religious liberals, as being crystallized to some extent without considerable possibilities for negotiation and easy compromises.

Nevertheless, there is some empirical indication of changes due to the aging process and/or the confrontation with new and challenging experiences. Several adolescents with conservative religious education may become more liberal, replacing literal interpretations with symbolic ones, as they progressively become young adults and/or enter higher education.[21] In parallel, there is some evidence that adults may also become more intense in their religiosity and spirituality as they become older,[22] and they may also become more conservative in their political attitudes.[23]

A final observation of interest to the understanding of the inertia regarding religious change is the fact that, across cultures, a weak but overall positive association exists between religiousness and sociomoral conservatism. In traditional societies, this extends further to a negative association between religiousness and the more basic and global personality dimension of (low) openness to experience.[24]

---

[20] Wiebke Bleidorn/Christopher J. Hopwood, Stability and Change in Personality Traits over the Lifespan, in: Dan P. McAdams/Rebecca L. Shiner/Jennifer L. Tackett (eds.), *Handbook of Personality Development*. New York: Guilford 2019, 237–252.

[21] Fritz K. Oser/W. George Scarlett/Anton Bucher, Religious and Spiritual Development Throughout the Life Span, in: William Damon/Richard L. Lerner (eds.), *Handbook of Child Psychology. Volume 1. Theoretical Models of Human Development*. Hoboken (NJ): Wiley ⁶2006, 942–998 for review.

[22] Paul Wink/Michele Dillon/Dan Farina, Religion, Spirituality, and the Agential Self, in: Dan P. McAdams/Rebecca L. Shiner/Jennifer L. Tacket (eds.), *Handbook of Personality Development*. New York: Guilford 2019, 364–379.

[23] Jonathan C. Peterson/Kevin B. Smith/John R. Hibbing, Do People Really Become More Conservative as They Age?, in: *The Journal of Politics* 82 (2/2020), 600–611.

[24] Vassilis Saroglou, Culture, Personality, and Religiosity, in: A. Timothy Church (ed.), *The Praeger Handbook of Personality Across Cultures. Volume 2*. Santa Barbara (CA): Praeger 2017, 153–184.

Thus, in many societies in the world today, especially in traditional societies, conservative religionists are a majority.[25] In modern secular societies, low openness to experience is characteristic only of religious fundamentalism, but not necessarily of mere religious belief and practice. In other words, within the latter societies, there is non-negligible variability among religionists regarding their propensity to consider or not consider change in the religious domain.[26]

5 Resistance to (Religious) Change: Underlying Factors

What are the factors that undermine religious change and favor resistance to change? Psychological research has identified a series of individual and situational factors that do not facilitate or may even prevent change, in general.[27] I will revisit these factors here, applying them to the religious context, and I will also describe specific factors that appear particularly salient for religion and religiousness.

5.1 Classic Individual and Situational Factors

Above, we mentioned the role of personality, mainly low openness to experience and related tendencies, which, associated with religiousness, particularly in traditional societies, inhibit the interest and propensity for religious change. In addition, older age is a factor known to favor resistance to change. And older adults are overrepresented among religious believers and especially among active religionists and members of religious communities.[28] Certainly, the fact of entering old age

---

[25] Kibeom Lee et al., Personality, Religion, and Politics: An Investigation in 33 Countries, in: *European Journal of Personality* 32 (2/2018), 100–115.
[26] Jochen E. Gebauer et al., Cross-Cultural Variations in Big Five Relationships With Religiosity: A Sociocultural Motives Perspective, in: *Journal of Personality and Social Psychology* 107 (6/2014), 1064–1091.
[27] See, for introductions and reviews: Eric B. Dent/Susan Galloway Goldberg, Challenging 'Resistance to Change', in: *Journal of Applied Behavioral Science* 35 (1/1999), 25–41; John T. Jost, Resistance to Change: A Social Psychological Perspective, in: *Social Research* 82 (3/2015), 607–636; Joseph R. Lao/Jason Young, *Resistance to Belief Change: Limits of Learning*. London/New York: Routledge 2020; and Shaul Oreg, Resistance to Change: Developing an Individual Differences Measure, in: *Journal of Applied Psychology* 88 (4/2003), 680–693.
[28] Pew Research Center, The Age Gap in Religion Around the World, on: Pew Research Center

is not necessarily accompanied by an increase of faith and practice – in fact, some older adults may even exit religion at that stage of life. Similarly, young adulthood is not necessarily a life period that leads to apostasy.[29] Nevertheless, some asymmetry exists in terms of age among religionists, with young adults being underrepresented. Older adults are also overrepresented among the high clergy, a body that can reasonably be perceived as being very vigilant regarding the maintenance of the many features of a given religion. Therefore, not surprisingly, age should not facilitate a propensity for religious change.

Beyond individual characteristics like age and personality, there are several situational factors that enhance humans' natural resistance to change. Organizations with a highly hierarchical and authoritarian structure are also reluctant to change. This is particularly the case when organizations do not make significant space for discursive processes that would allow for self-reflection, criticism, and reconsideration of things. Indeed, many religions, denominations, and religious communities are characterized by a clear, even rigid, hierarchical structure and by the unwillingness to give discursive processes legitimate authority. An example from the Christian Orthodox Churches may be significant. Though explicitly promoting synodality as the Church's system of governance at all levels, from the parish level to the Panorthodox Synod level, these Churches have been heavily criticized by internal actors – typically lay theologians and lower-rank clergy but not bishops – for the considerable dysfunction of the synodal system at various levels.[30] In such contexts, authority is concentrated in the hands of one person, i.e., the Primate of a local Church, or the body of bishops. Interestingly, some bishops recently added the term 'and episcopal' (καί ιεραρχικόν) when referring to the 'synodal' (συνοδικόν) system of the Church's governance. Not surprisingly, the Orthodox Churches are those that have been marked by minimal change, if any, compared to the Catholic and Protestant Churches and communities.

Furthermore, resistance to change is particularly strong in societal contexts where people, especially key actors, are unprepared for change and may even lack the competence to imagine and implement change. To remain with the same religious context of the Christian Orthodox Churches, which I am quite familiar with: the religious authorities seem to have little perception of the need for change,

---

(13.06.2018), URL: https://www.pewresearch.org/religion/2018/06/13/the-age-gap-in-religion-around-the-world/ (30.03.2023).
29 Paul Wink/Michele Dillon/Dan Farina, Religion, Spirituality, and the Agential Self, in: Dan P. McAdams/Rebecca L. Shiner/Jennifer L. Tacket (eds.), *Handbook of Personality Development*. New York: Guilford 2019, 364–379.
30 Stavros Yangazoglou (ed.), Συνοδικότητα καί ὁμοφωνία [Conciliarity and Consensus] [Special section], in: *Θεολογία 86* (2/2015), 3–194.

not necessarily because of unwillingness, but partly due to lack of knowledge and subsequent incompetence. For instance, their familiarity with human and social sciences in general, and human and social sciences of religion in particular, is particularly weak. In fact, among religions and religious denominations, there is an implicit hierarchy regarding the familiarity with human and social sciences. For instance, mainstream Protestantism and contemporary Catholicism have experienced important openness to these sciences. This, in turn, has had an impact, for instance, on the historical and critical approaches of the sacred texts or the consideration of the ways to assume pastoral responsibilities and understand traditional religious practice and norms. The opposite has been the case for religions and denominations that are unaware of and indifferent with regard to the knowledge accumulated by scientists of religion – this seems to be particularly the case today in Orthodox Christianity and Islam.

Resistance to change is also strong when the key actors are simply unaware of the need for change, are sitting in a zone of comfort, and thus have poor motivation to change. For instance, in countries with a religious monopole, i.e., with one religion or denomination being highly predominant, religious expressions are typically traditional, rather immutable, and not really negotiable.[31] Countries with a still vibrant Western Christian tradition like Poland, and especially (all) countries of Eastern Christian tradition, dispose of religious authorities who feel too comfortable within a society where religiousness looks natural and is part of the collective identity. Religionists and religious leaders may thus be hostile against secularism, religious diversity, and the associated need for change. On the contrary, in contexts with high religious and convictional diversity, including those where believers and non-believers coexist as important segments of the society, religious beliefs, rituals, norms, and institutions experience considerable internal developments.[32]

Low trust of leaders may be another factor that diminishes the propensity for change. Even when leaders propose well-justified, meaningful, and pertinent changes, followers may be reluctant to welcome such changes because of a generalized distrust of these leaders by the members. Within the Christian Orthodox world, an interesting example of this process is, in my opinion, the current opposition that very active religious believers and practitioners show against any change proposed by ecclesiastic authorities, even very secondary changes regarding minor aspects of the ritual and the tradition. Since there is a cleavage in these religionists' minds between power- and career-oriented religious leaders on the one hand,

---

31 Vassilis Saroglou/Vanessa Delpierre/Rebecca Dernelle, Values and Religiosity: a Meta-analysis of Studies Using Schwartz's Model, in: *Personality and Individual Differences* 37 (4/2004), 721–734.
32 Pippa Norris/Ronald Inglehart, *Sacred and Secular*.

and ascetic excellence and authentic spirituality of famous monastic figures on the other hand, any change proposed by the former is typically confronted with high resistance. This factor partly explains, in my opinion, why decades of formal ecumenical dialogue has had almost zero effect on important segments of the Christian Orthodox world which have remained hostile toward Western Christian Churches. The Orthodox participation in this dialog has been almost exclusively left in the hands of ecclesiastic authorities and their close theologian experts.

Finally, ironically, too many changes may be an obstacle for new change due to exhaustion. Individuals, groups, and organizations are not programmed to change constantly; they also need periods of continuity and calmness. Large organizations in particular need time for all members to assimilate change and develop the experience of continuity beyond the changes they have experienced. For instance, Vatican II has created a series of important and impactful changes within Catholicism – possibly with some costs, even if these costs are minor compared to the greater benefits. Subsequently, new important proposed changes in the Catholic Church, like accentuating synodality in the Church's governance to the highest degree or allowing women to enter priesthood, may be too 'onerous' to be implemented in the period following the many Vatican II-related developments.

5.2 Religion-Specific Factors of Resistance to Change

As stated earlier in this work, the idea that truth pre-exists as a whole within a given religion, rather than being a reality to be fully discovered in the future, is by itself a major factor undermining the propensity for religious change. In the least, it pushes for religious change that is primarily an adaptation that contributes to a more accurate consideration of that truth. This conception is further consolidated within those religions that claim some kind of infallibility, be it located in a text, a person, or an institution. Of course, infallibility is often complemented by a source of counter-power: for instance, *reception* by the community is considered as important for the acceptance of a specific synod's infallibility. Nevertheless, the mere idea of the existence of some kind and location of infallibility is sufficient to make religious changes particularly difficult.

Furthermore, at least within monotheistic traditions, religious beliefs, ritual, norms, and institutional functioning are typically conceived as a well-integrated whole with a strong internal coherence. Consequently, even a change in one minor aspect of the whole, such as an update to the interpretation of a given belief, the modification of a feature in a particular ritual, or the replacement of an old rule with a new one in the life of the community, needs to be made in a way that will not disturb – or will not be perceived as disturbing – the other parts that constitute the coherent whole. In other words, religions characterized by high integralism may have particular difficulties in implementing changes because of the interconnection between all aspects of belief and practice.

In line with the ideas of pre-existing truth, infallibility, and integralism, religions endorse certain beliefs and use a specific rhetoric that allow contradictions to be minimized and serve the well-known psychological need to resolve cognitive dissonance. The latter is the need to reduce and extinguish the discrepancy in individuals' minds between their ideas that may be divergent and contradictory with each other; the same can be said for the discrepancies between their ideas and acts, and between their acts. For instance, how can the religious community reduce cognitive dissonance when errors and failures become evident? A helpful idea is the belief that the religious community is glorious and eternal. Such a belief implies the minimization, if not denial, of failures and errors, including those within the moral domain: since the Church is invincible and will persist for ever, failures are only accidents and do not potentially threaten the existence of the community. This may be an erroneous estimation if one takes the historical fact into account that religions can die. It is of importance to note that the endorsement of the idea that quality is more important than quantity minimizes the risk the decrease in membership (e.g., due to secularization) may have for the maintenance of the community: despite significant losses, the community will be eternal. Obviously, these perceptions do not produce pressure to consider potential changes.

Another, subtler, rhetorical strategy is the propagation of the idea that the positive things, acts, and accomplishments are produced by the glorious Church, whereas the errors, failures, and sins are committed by the 'sons and the daughters of the Church.' This denotes the psychological defense mechanism of projecting the bad self to the outside. A related defense mechanism is the development of the idea that negative considerations about aspects of a given religion in general, or at specific moments of its life, are due to external sources of unjustified criticism. These sources, such as the media and some politicians, are usually considered immoral or by definition hostile to religion. The fact that several empirical studies, even before the Covid-19 pandemic, have shown that individual religiousness is positively associated with an endorsement of conspiracy beliefs,[33] and not only in very traditional

---

[33] Paweł Łowicki et al., Does Religion Predict Coronavirus Conspiracy Beliefs? Centrality of Religiosity, Religious Fundamentalism, and COVID-19 Conspiracy Beliefs, in: *Personality and Individual Differences 187* (2022), Article 111413 and Gordon Pennycook et al., On the Belief That Beliefs Should Change According to Evidence: Implications for Conspiratorial, Moral, Paranormal, Political, Religious, and Science Beliefs, in: *Judgment and Decision Making 15* (4/2020), 476–498.

societies but also in secularized Western countries,[34] reveals the importance of this mentality: the evil fights the faithful people from inside, but also from outside.

A final factor, inherent to religious communities, that works to discourage change is the risk for schisms. The history of most, possibly all, religions is simultaneously a history of their schisms. Leaders of dynamic and lively religions that want to prevent a significant decrease of their membership and the long-term effects of disunity are very attentive to avoid decisions that may facilitate internal schisms. Undoubtedly, implementing changes constitutes such an important risk. Disunity is a cause of suffering, and schisms raise doubts about the value and validity of the original religion. In addition, a drastic decrease in membership is a subtle reminder that religious beliefs are fragile assertions: their uncertainty and independence from any kind of objective proof need to be compensated by a significant number of coreligionists who attest together that these beliefs, embraced by many, should somehow be true.

Therefore, religious communities most often live under the threat of their most conservative or fundamentalist segments, which may depart from the community if they deem that significant changes have been implemented. One can even consider the fundamentalist tendencies within established religions as being animated essentially by a propensity for competition for the greatest possible purity: the most authentic spiritual father, parish, bishop, movement, etc. will be the one that adopts the strictest standards in their religious expression. (Although less frequent, the direction may be the opposite, with the liberal segments initiating schisms). Religious leaders are thus often obliged to maintain a subtle equilibrium between conservative and liberal voices. They most often choose the equilibrium that will preserve some sort of consensus – not necessarily what they themselves believe as being the best. Undoubtedly, the constant search for consensus is not the best way to encourage change.

6 Summary and Conclusion

In this work, I examined several key issues regarding the interplay between religious continuity and religious change, by focusing mainly on religiousness, i.e., people's experience of religion through beliefs, rituals, norms, and community. Going

---

[34] Inga Jasinskaja-Lahti/Jolanda Jetten, Unpacking the Relationship Between Religiosity and Conspiracy Beliefs in Australia, in: *British Journal of Social Psychology 58* (4/2019), 938–954 and Natasha Galliford/Aadrian Furnham, Individual Difference Factors and Beliefs in Medical and Political Conspiracy Theories, in: *Scandinavian Journal of Psychology 58* (5/2017), 422–428.

beyond the simple idea that, similar to all living entities, religion both remains the same and changes, it appears that religious continuity, not to say sameness, is strong, certainly stronger than that of many other domains of human activity. This is of course mainly due to the very nature of religiousness as an attachment and fidelity to a fundamental and foundational past truth and thus is not restricted to conservative and fundamentalist religious expressions.

The substantial impact of continuity limits the possibilities for change and shapes religious change, which, after a close examination of some examples from empirical research, appears to be more limited and discrete than experts adopting a micro approach may think. Here, I used the examples of the relationships of individual religiousness with humor, sexuality, homophobia, and intergroup prejudice. Though some changes have been observed, indicating that religious changes parallel and follow societal changes, the continuation is striking. This poses, among others, the question of how to explain the discrepancy between theological and ecclesiastic developments on the one hand and non-negligible stability in the way people's religiousness functions in everyday life on the other hand. Here, I proposed at least three explanations: delay between theory and practice of change, overestimation of change by experts, and defensive rhetoric to give the illusion of change.

A further examination of the diversity of the representations people have of change, and thus the diversity of the underlying models of change, suggested that religious change is initiated and experienced mainly as an adaptation to societal changes and as acculturation to new cultural contexts. Thus, religious change is much more restrained compared to other models of change such as change of direction, progress, timely necessity, replacement, or full transformation. As a consequence, very often, religion either implies continuity and sameness despite claiming change; or, on the contrary, it implements change under the guise of continuity and slight adaptation. Nevertheless, discrete and restricted religious change within the constraints of heavy continuity implicitly activates the idea that time and mutability denote human imperfection, and thus change may be an alteration.

How do religion and religiousness change – when is this the case? Though it is risky to advance the idea that religious changes have a direction, I argued that both directions are possible, with religiousness potentially becoming more liberal, individualized, autonomous, and thus intrinsic in motivation, or, on the contrary, more traditional, conservative, and conformist in motivation. However, as shown by an impressive number of studies focusing especially on the moderating role that societal developments and secularism play on religiousness, the evidence favors the idea that the big picture does not point to rigidification of believers and polarization between them and secularists. Religiousness, at least within major religions that have adapted to survive, follows societal changes, though with some delay.

And the differences between believers and non-believers appear greater in secular compared to traditional societies due to nonbelievers' liberalization, not due to the hypothetical rigidification of believers.

All kinds of societal and cultural changes constitute external sources of religious change. These include changes in the domains of politics, economy, health, education, law, science, ethics, mobility, natural disasters, conflicts, and war, among others. In parallel, or independently, sources internal to religion may cause change – any kind of religious change. Theological and ecclesiastic developments may generate changes, but most importantly charismatic religious figures, prophetic voices, founders of new movements or new religions, often in opposition to the institutional authorities or the dominant traditions, initiate change and bring significant developments to the landscape of world religions. In addition, interindividual variability, among people in general, and thus among religionists and religious leaders in particular, with regard to the personality disposition for either high or low openness to new, diverse, challenging, and complex ideas, values, acts, and experiences, as well as the intra-individual stability of these personality tendencies, guarantee the persistence of the battle between religious conservatives and religious liberals, as well as the continuous interplay between continuity or sameness on one hand and change or adaptation on the other hand.

Finally, there are plethora of well-known factors that enhance humans' natural tendency to resist change. Many of them also apply to the religious context. Beyond individual factors like age (across religious cultures, older adults, less open to change, are typically overrepresented) and personality disposition for low openness to experience (conservatives are overrepresented among religionists, especially in traditional countries), we can note several relevant situational factors. These include an unawareness of the need for change, an unpreparedness for change, a lack of competence, poor motivation to change when living in comfortable societal environments, simple exhaustion from previous changes, a hierarchical and authoritarian structure, and non-valorization of discursive processes, but also a lack of trust of the organization's leaders when the latter try to implement meaningful changes.

In addition to the factors mentioned above, one can describe specific internal features of religion that amplify the natural tendency to resist change. I have presented several that seemed critical: the idea of infallibility, the belief that the group is glorious and eternal, the strong integralism characterizing at least the monotheistic traditions, several rhetorical strategies that facilitate the reduction of cognitive dissonance when facing important failures and errors in the community, and finally the fear of (new) schisms. The latter, among others, is strategically used as a threat by conservative and fundamentalist segments in order to oppose the implementation of change.

At the end of this initial exploration of the understudied topic of religion and change, at least from the perspective of the behavioral sciences of religion, I would like to mention a limitation of the present work. An important area where, within religion, it is believed that significant changes are implemented is that of the ascetic and monastic life, at least for religions that include these forms of religious life. From the believer's perspective, it is assumed that these modes of life contribute to more internal and more gradual personal transformations. Moreover, these internal transformations are perceived as bringing about, albeit indirectly and progressively, external changes and transformation of the world. These assumptions may not be purely idealistic elaborations and pose interesting questions that can be empirically investigated. Nevertheless, relevant empirical research on this issue is lacking and thus it may be premature and risky to make any empirical statement confirming or infirming these interesting assumptions here.

To conclude the present work, I would like to claim that of intellectual intrigue is less the question of how religion succeeds to preserve sameness despite implementing some kind of change, at least as adaptation. Rather, for the scientists of religion, the more challenging and perhaps fascinating question seems to be how religions succeed to cultivate a feeling of uninterrupted continuity and true fidelity while at the same time they introduce gradual and progressive, sometimes even radical, changes within the religious landscape.

Guy G. Stroumsa

The Study of Religion and the Spirit of Orientalism: Cultural Transformations and Scholarly Shifts

Like all social institutions, religions constantly change, evolving and transforming themselves. Sometimes, when one can speak of brutal transformations and of religious revolutions, this truism is obvious to all.[1] But more often, the conatus of religions entails their more or less 'peaceful' evolution. Now, while all religions have a potential for radical transformation in their DNA, they are instinctively more inclined toward conservatism, and the function of their hermeneutical systems, while permitting change when deemed necessary or unavoidable, consists essentially in slowing down the pace of such change, and making sure, it goes unnoticed, or *almost* unnoticed. Daniel Kahneman, a psychologist who won a Nobel Prize in economics, has shown that we all function with two parallel systems of thought: 'Thinking, Fast and Slow,' as he entitled his book on the topic. Similarly, I propose we identify two alternate patterns of religious change: slow versus fast. Religion and society at large, then, are complementary motors, actors, and objects of change in history. In a permanent dialectical relationship with one another, religion and society are taking turns at initiating change, responding to it, modulating it, and transforming the direction, intensity, and even the very nature of this change.

In a recently published book, The Idea of Semitic Monotheism: The Rise and Fall of a Scholarly Myth, I sought to understand some societal dimensions of the idea of Semitic monotheism, an idea coined by Ernest Renan in the mid-19th century and developed in European scholarship in the subsequent decades. This idea was interdependent with both new perceptions of Judaism and Islam and transformed attitudes toward Jews and Muslims. Hence, I tried to highlight various veiled connections between the history of religions, then a growing scholarly discipline, and some deep changes in European societies, related to secularization processes. I shall present a few preliminary reflections on this research here, which, I think, bear directly on the topic of our conference, from a particular but capital angle.

It barely needs mentioning that since the early modern Great Discoveries,

---

[1] This text was read (on zoom) as a keynote lecture at the Conference of the European Academy of Religion in Münster on September 1, 2021. I wish to thank Professor Hans-Peter Grosshans for his kind invitation to deliver the lecture. The text is adapted from the introduction to my Guy G. Stroumsa, *The Idea of Semitic Monotheism. The Rise and Fall of a Scholarly Myth*. Oxford: Oxford University Press 2021.

and especially since the industrial revolution, the pace of change has been faster than ever before. The contemporary entry into the Digital Age has transformed the world, indeed is still transforming it in many ways, into what we have learned to call a 'global village', although a thoroughly polluted one, far from any idyllic or Romantic imagination. With the Enlightenment, in particular, Europe, and then many societies all around the world, have undergone a complex process of heightened secularization – a process jump-started by the Reformation. While secularization is a highly polyvalent term, it always refers to a shrinking of the status of established or organized religion in the public sphere, including personal law, the limitation of its political role, and the enhanced focus of the private and personal sphere as the main or legitimate locus of religion. It is clear, then, that the process of secularization has a deep impact on the nature of religion, involving far-reaching changes first in its practice but also in its doctrine as well as in its self-perception.

With those changes in religion, another, perhaps subtler but no less significant phenomenon was initiated by the critique of religion at the time of the Enlightenment. The non-theological approach of Christianity, and by extension of Judaism and Islam, the other monotheistic religions best known in Europe, also permitted the growth of the modern study of religion, and modeled anew the approach to religious phenomena. I wish to argue that a major paradigm shift in the very perception of monotheism, and in particular of Judaism and Islam, occurred throughout the 19th century, and that this paradigm shift bears directly on the formation of modern scholarship on religion.

Towards the end of the 19th century, the 'science of religion' stood (unlike in our own days) at the forefront of knowledge, and its claims were so many combative statements, which impacted on society at large. The broader, public significance of a discipline usually perceived today as arcane, is one of the themes I hope to showcase here. The modern study of religion developed throughout the 19th century, up to the establishment, in its last third, of the first academic chairs, journals, and conferences exclusively devoted to the new discipline. To a great extent, it focused then on the religious systems of newly discovered peoples, throughout Asia, in the Americas, and in Africa, as well as on those from Mediterranean and Near Eastern Antiquity, which were now analyzed thanks to new philological tools and the supporting evidence brought by archaeology. In this context, the understanding of polytheistic (or, as in the case of Buddhism, non-theistic) systems, approached for the first time in a non-polemical fashion, *sine ira et studio*, played a central role.

In medieval Christian societies, both in Byzantium and in the Latin West, there existed a single taxonomy of the world's religions.[2] For a full millennium, roughly

---

2 On early Christian taxonomies of religions, see Francesco Massa, Nommer et classer les religions

from the 8th to the 18th century, Christian thinkers had perceived the world as divided between four main religious families: Christianity, Judaism, Islam, and 'the rest', also known as 'heathenism'. As a rule, this fourfold taxonomy did not entail the existence of a 'Triple Alliance' of sorts between the monotheistic traditions. Rather, polemics remained the usual medium of communication between them. Christianity (or, more precisely, its various orthodox versions) was of course the only true religion (*vera religio* in Augustine's terms), while Judaism and Islam were considered to be erroneous ones (*falsae religiones*), one upstream and one downstream of Christianity, as it were. From Epiphanius of Salamis to John of Damascus, Patristic heresiologists could even present them as heresies of sorts, Judaism being the first heresy and Islam the last – and worst – one.[3] In different ways, Jews and Muslims remained the enemies of the true faith. But as monotheists, Jews and Muslims alike were recognized to be akin, in a deep sense, to the Christians, despite the enormous difference between them in Christian perception. While Jews were generally tolerated (and humiliated, as children of the devil [John 8:44]) in traditional Christian societies, Muslims typically remained the enemy without.[4]

In modern times, the discovery of new societies and their traditional cultures demanded that this classification be abandoned, as the sole category of 'heathenism' was no longer adequate to interpret the great variety of religions in the world. When the old taxonomy was abandoned, the centuries-old family relationship (to use Wittgenstein's metaphor) between the three monotheistic religions became significantly weakened. When William Jones, speaking in 1786 at the recently founded Calcutta Asiatic Society, announced that he had discovered similarities between Sanskrit, Greek, and Latin, he was launching a new classification of languages and peoples, which would quickly become the main paradigm, beyond linguistics, for a number of disciplines, throughout the 19th century. Semites and Aryans now took the traditional place of the offspring of Shem and Japheth, two of Noah's three sons.[5] To a great extent, the Semites were imagined through the

---

aux IIe–IVe siècles: la taxonomie 'paganisme, judaïsme, christianisme', in: *Revue de l'histoire des religions 234* (2017), 689–715.
3 The transformation of Judaism into a Christian heresy is of course less intuitive than the Christian perception of the earliest Islam as a heresy. But Epiphanius explicitly called Judaism a heresy, while Justinian's rulings can be said to treat the Jews as heretics. See Guy G. Stroumsa, *The Making of the Abrahamic Religions in Late Antiquity*. Oxford: Oxford University Press 2015, 175–188.
4 Judaism and Islam did not always reciprocate the compliment paid to them by Christianity, as Jewish and Muslim medieval thinkers rarely considered Christianity to be monotheistic.
5 Throughout history, Ham, Noah's third son, traditionally identified with blackness, has remained the incarnation of blacks and slaves. See Benjamin Braude, Cham et Noé. Race, esclavage et exégèse entre islam, judaïsme et christianisme, in: *Annales. Histoire, Sciences Sociales 57* (2002), 93–125, as

model of the Hebrews (and the Jews; indeed, from the 1880s on, the newly-coined word 'anti-Semitism' never referred to anyone except the Jews), while the Greeks represented the focal model of the Aryans. Monotheism would now often be conceived as a characteristic of a postulated ancient Semitic religion, while polytheism, would usually be identified as pertaining to the nature of the Aryan religion. This new paradigm gave the old taxonomy the *coup de grâce*. New categories had to be forged, and this was one of the major tasks of the new 'science of religion'. A Europe whose identity was perceived as torn between the Semitic roots of its religion and the Aryan nature of its languages and ethnicities saw the emergence of a new and deep ambivalence to monotheism. This ambivalence was echoing and amplifying those trends in the radical Enlightenment that had grown strongly critical of the established churches.

The new European discovery of similarities between Sanskrit and almost all European languages led to the identification of families of languages and also of families of religions, in particular the Aryan and the Semitic religious families.[6] Deducing religion (and ethnicity) from linguistics is, of course, a fallacy, a fact underlined toward the end of the 19th century by the French polymath Salomon Reinach in his long article 'Le mirage oriental' – a fallacy which, as we know, would have dramatic consequences.[7] A number of significant European intellectuals now started to identify European languages and peoples as belonging to the Indo-European (or Indo-Germanic in German parlance) or Aryan family. They were loath to consider their own religion, Christianity, as related in any significant way to Judaism and Islam, the main extant Semitic religions, and preferred to see in it a religious expression of the Aryan race. To be sure, one should not overstate the global importance of pan-Aryanism and imagine that it represented the leading trend in 19th-century European thought. The majority among their contemporaries did not take the most vociferous heralds of this kind of racialism seriously. To deduct the early nature of racialist thought patterns from its radical, murderous

---

well as David M. Goldenberg, *The Curse of Ham. Race and Slavery in Early Judaism, Christianity and Islam*. Princeton/Oxford: Princeton University Press 2005.

6 Maurice Olender, *The Languages of Paradise. Race, Religion, and Philology in the Nineteenth Century*. Cambridge (MA): Harvard University Press 1992 [French original: Les langues du paradis. Aryens et Sémites: un couple providentiel. Paris: Gallimard/Le Seuil 1989]. Olender discusses some of the figures we shall encounter in the following chapters, such as Ernest Renan, Max Müller, and Ignaz Goldziher.

7 Salomon Reinach, Le mirage oriental, in: *L'anthropologie 4* (1893), 539–579 and 699. See Chapter 10 below. For another use of this metaphor: see Louis Bertrand, La réalité et le Mirage oriental, in: *Revue des Deux Mondes 48* [5e période] (1908), 139–172. Bertrand later published a novel entitled *Le mirage oriental* (Paris: Perrin, 1920).

consequences in the 20th century would amount to teleological reasoning. Nevertheless, in the academic study of religion the Aryan-Semite taxonomy did have a major formative role.[8]

Paradoxically or not, Christianity itself remained relatively peripheral to the development of the new discipline. It is always easier to develop the distance needed for an objective and critical approach toward the religions of others, rather than toward one's own. Indeed, while the traditional reflection on religion had been the object of theology and philosophy, the modern study of religion grew mainly at the interface of philology, oriental studies, and ethnology. The religion of Biblical Israel stayed within the purview of theology, while post-biblical and Rabbinic Judaism were usually considered of little interest, reflecting the religious decadence that in Christian perception had occurred among the Hebrews after the biblical prophets, and certainly since Jesus. Moreover, the historical study of Christianity and the critical, philological approach to the Bible in our period remained largely in the hands of liberal Protestant theologians; Catholics were still forbidden by ecclesiastical authorities to deal with higher biblical criticism.

The study of Islam, on the other hand, continued to be mainly in the hands of Arabists, who, for centuries, had typically displayed a disparaging attitude to Muhammad, dubbed a false prophet, and to his religion. As a result, Judaism, Christianity, and Islam did not form part of the new discipline's core. My primary goal here is to appreciate the consequences of this fact for the study of monotheism, in particular on the scholarly approaches to Judaism and Islam, two religions that eventually came to be perceived as quite alien to Christian Europe. Attitudes to Judaism and to Islam, however, stayed strikingly different from one another, as Judaism was perceived as the more intimate enemy, the enemy within, as it were, while Islam remained essentially foreign, extraneous. Moreover, in most countries of Western Europe, there existed numerous old Jewish communities, which were being emancipated in the 19th century. There were very few Muslims then, and no Muslim communities in those areas. This discrepancy also partly explains the difference in the intensity of attitudes towards Judaism and Islam.

In contradistinction to the old, abstract history of ideas, intellectual history seeks to understand ideas within their full social and political context. When dealing with approaches to religion in the 19th century, accelerated secularization, growing nationalism, and imperial colonialism provide the immediate context. The analysis of scholarly discourse on religion must reflect the new status of religion in societies that were undergoing intensive processes of secularization. On the one

---

[8] See Stefan Arvidsson, *Aryan Idols. Indo-European Mythology as Ideology and Science*. Chicago: Chicago University Press 2006.

hand, with the industrial revolution and the growth of cities, the working classes were learning to free themselves from ecclesiastical control, and the traditional or established churches were losing their customary grip on Western European societies. On the other hand, a number of powerful thinkers, pursuing the radical Enlightenment's onslaught on traditional Christianity, were in search of new forms of spirituality. From Hegel's age of the Spirit to Auguste Comte's religion of the future, their proposals seduced many, such as Friedrich David Strauss in Germany or Edgar Quinet in France. The second half of the century saw important decline in the number of church goers, together with the growth of the historical and comparative study of religion.[9]

Expressions of religion were regressing from the public sphere to the private one. The Christian dimension of European identities, of course, was in no way disappearing. Rather, the semiotic range of Christianity moved, as it was increasingly transformed from the expression of Europe's core *religious* identity to representing a central element of European *cultural* memory. This was perhaps nowhere manifested as clearly as in the case of the Bible in Protestant countries, where, in the 19th century, it became in its vernacular translations, a core element of education and culture, of what the Germans call Bildung.[10] Even though Christianity did not always represent actual shared beliefs and practices, it certainly remained at the core of historical consciousness and national identity. This is what Hegel referred to as the transformation, or *Aufhebung* of Christianity in the full-fledged *Geist*.[11]

Secularization alone, however, does not explain the transformation of the status of Christianity in European consciousness from representing Europe's religious capital to its cultural capital – to use a concept crafted by the French sociologist Pierre Bourdieu. Both the rapid growth of nationalism and the expansion of colonial conquests in the age of imperialism must be factored in. The growing feelings of European superiority versus Asian and African peoples and cultures would, in the second half of the century, in the heyday of colonialism, be expressed in a new key, that of 'scientific racism'. The new expression of disparaging attitudes to foreign peoples and their cultures would have an immediate, potent, and lasting impact upon scholarly conceptions. Among others, Martin Bernal, focusing on the

---

[9] For an analytical description of the period, see Owen Chadwick, *The Secularization of the European Mind in the Nineteenth Century*. Cambridge: Cambridge University Press 1975.

[10] See Jonathan Sheehan, *The Enlightenment Bible. Translation, Scholarship, Culture*. Princeton: Princeton University Press 2005. Cf. Chapter 3, note 8.

[11] See for instance Jean-Claude Monod, *La querelle de la sécularisation de Hegel à Blumenberg*. Paris: Vrin 2002. On the relationship between philosophical and theological perceptions of secularization, see Hans Blumenberg, *Säkularisierung und Selbstbehauptung*. Frankfurt: Suhrkamp 1974.

study of Greek antiquity, has shown how the categories forged in 19th century scholarship reflected racist ideas.[12]

One paradoxical and insidious consequence of this distantiation from Judaism and Islam led to a major fracture in European identity and to a new crisis of European consciousness, following that of the Enlightenment, so masterly analyzed by Paul Hazard.[13] The depth of this fracture, as well as its effect on the status of Judaism and Islam in the European mind, has yet to be fully measured.[14]

Before the Enlightenment, the Near East (then usually referred to as simply 'the East'), was considered to be the soil of all human religious origins. All religions had come from the Ancient Near East, from Egypt to Babylonia, through the lands of the Bible.[15] As Christianity was perceived, essentially, as the European religion par excellence, Judaism and Islam were, for the European mind, the two surviving religions from the Ancient Near East. Now, however, they became perceived only as coming from the East of the West, or as the West of the deep and true East, that of India and China. Judaism and Islam thus fell between Europe and India, between the two poles of Indo-European cultural and religious creativity. To be sure, scholars recognized that the geographical spread of Islam throughout the world was impressive, and that both Jews and Muslims believed in one God. Yet, all in all, racial prejudice against the Jews (distinct from traditional religious anti-Semitism) and condescending attitudes to Islam and Islamic societies entailed a strong devaluation of both Judaism and Islam and a clear preference for Indo-European religious systems and cultural traditions over Semitic religions and cultures. European Christians were thus contriving to escape the Jewish, Near-Eastern origins of their religion. The close relationship of Christianity with European culture, it was argued, did not deny its universal nature, and it was therefore Europe's duty to promote Christianity throughout Asia and Africa, along the model of its earlier conquests in the Americas.

---

12 Martin Bernal, *Black Athena. The Afroasiatic Roots of Classical Civilization. Volume I: The Fabrication of Ancient Greece 1785–1985*. New Brunswick (NJ): Rutgers University Press 1987; Bernal has insisted on the major role played by the intensification of racism and the central importance of 'ethnicity' as a principle of historical explanation. He was able to show the crucial part they played in the formation of new taxonomies opposing 'Aryans' to 'Semites'.
13 Paul Hazard, *The Crisis of the European Mind. 1680–1715*. New York: New York Review of Books 2013 [French original: La crise de la conscience européenne. 1680–1715. Paris: Fayard 1961 [1935]].
14 Markus Messling, *Gebeugter Geist. Rassismus und Erkenntnis in der modernen europäischen Philologie*. Göttingen: Wallerstein 2016.
15 See for instance Guy G. Stroumsa, John Selden et les origines de l'orientalisme, in: Quentin Epron (ed.), *John Selden: juriste européen, Annuaire de l'Institut Michel Villey* (2012), 1–11.

Intellectual perceptions of Judaism and Islam, moreover, are directly related to social attitudes toward Jews and Muslims in European societies – a point which there is surely no need to belabor. In the early stages of Jewish emancipation (a process that had started with the French Revolution), Jewish communities in Western European societies were being transformed very fast. Together with emancipation and less exclusion from society at large came new tensions. The traditional forms of Christian anti-Judaism, which, of course, had not disappeared, were reactivated, as it were, in a new, racial key, and fresh forms of prejudice were formulated. In various ways, the Jews were now felt to be more alien than at any previous time. Their identity was perceived as an Asian one. In other words, the Jews did not really belong to Europe. Thus Herder, and so many after him.

At the same time, Islam was identified as the religion of Europe's immediate and scorned neighbor, the Ottoman Empire, and that of colonized peoples, from the Maghreb to the Indian subcontinent and beyond. As a consequence, Muslims were often despised and hated. For generations, there had existed, of course, significant Muslim communities on European soil, mainly in the Balkans. In southern European imagery, they were often pictured as peaceful traders. More often than not, however, they remained marginalized in Western European perception. Imperialism and colonialism, in Africa, the Near East, and South East Asia, could only strengthen negative attitudes toward Islam and Muslims and reactivate existing prejudices. Orientalist trends in art and literature, as we know, highlighted such negative attitudes towards Islam and Muslims in the 19th century.

In the mid-19th century, the French historian and philosopher Edgar Quinet coined the phrase 'la Renaissance orientale', by which he meant the new European scholarly interest in, and cultural sensitivity for, the civilizations of Asia.[16] Since Quinet's days, European perceptions of the Orient have remained a highly loaded topic, as demonstrated by the fate of Edward Said's *Orientalism*, a book published more than a generation ago, which soon became a cult book.[17] Over the years since its publication, polemics around it, at times in stringent tones, seem to remain endemic. There is no need to rehash either the important points it was making, or the detailed criticism of its various shortcomings here.[18] One of the deplorable

---

[16] Edgar Quinet, *Du génie des religions*. Paris: Charpentier 1842, 65–77. A century later, the literary scholar Raymond Schwab would use the expression as the title of his masterpiece, *La Renaissance orientale*. Paris: Payot 2014 [English translation: The Oriental Renaissance. Europe's Rediscovery of India and the East, 1680–1880. New York: Columbia University Press 1984].
[17] Edward Said, *Orientalism*. New York: Random House 1978.
[18] Cf. Robert Irwin, *For Lust of Knowing. The Orientalists and their Enemies*. London: Penguin 2006, 3–5. On the vitriolic polemics to which the book gave birth, see for instance the exchange between Said and two distinguished Arabists and Islamic scholars, Oleg Grabar and Bernard Lewis,

consequences of Said's book, however, is of direct import to our topic, as it derided the colossal effort made by many bright, studious, and courageous scholars. They succeeded in opening new vistas to whole civilizations far beyond the borders of Europe. Intellectual curiosity, among these scholars, seems to have been boundless. A number of excellent monographs on aspects of 19th-century Orientalism have done much to highlight its rich and complex history, as well as the many links, both obvious (starting with linguistic demands) and implicit, between Orientalism and the study of religion.

While the study of Islam and that of Judaism form part of the Orientalist enterprise (and I use this word without its usual pejorative connotations), they obviously also belong to the study of religion. Like Orientalism, the latter grew throughout the 19th century, eventually becoming a full-fledged scholarly discipline. How and when was the modern, critical study of religion born? Among the branches of humanistic scholarship, the study of religion seems to have particularly suffered from a lack of reflexivity upon its own history.[19] In the last generation, however, sophisticated histories of the history of religion have done much to remedy this sore state of affairs, shedding new light on the history of the modern study of religion. It is but natural that these books usually focus on the second half of the 19th century, the period when the first university chairs and scholarly journals were established in a number of European countries. In countries of Protestant culture in particular, the study of religion became established in theological faculties. One of the major consequences of this situation is that the study of religion long remained deeply embedded in theological conceptions, as Jonathan Z. Smith was able to show regarding the religions of late antiquity and the world of Early Christianity.[20]

What is needed is a critical genealogy of scholarly discourse. In a way, such a genealogy would attempt to unveil the unconscious of the discipline.[21] By 'unconscious', I refer to implicit, hidden principles that dictate research and the development of the field. It is no accident that such principles usually remain unex-

---

in *The New York Review of Books* (issue of August 12, 1982). Quite oddly, the polemics continues unabated, more than forty years after the publication of *Orientalism*. See for instance Adam Shatz, 'Orientalism,' Then and Now, in: The New York Review (20.05.2019), URL: https://www.nybooks.com/daily/2019/05/20/orientalism-then-and-now/ (21.07.2022).
19 Robert Orsi, The 'So-Called History' of the Study of Religion, in: *Method and Theory in the Study of Religion* 20 (2008), 134–138: 'The past of religious studies has been until recently largely invisible...' (134).
20 Jonathan Z. Smith, *Drudgery Divine. On the Comparison of Early Christianities and the Religions of Late Antiquity*. Chicago: University of Chicago Press 1990.
21 This is to be distinguished from the point made by Philippe Borgeaud, *Aux origines de l'histoire des religions*. Paris: Seuil 2004, 18, on religions representing the unconscious of civilizations.

pressed, in the field of religion, perhaps, more than anywhere else. If Freud is right in arguing that religion is particularly fraught with repression (*Verdrängung*), the same may also be true of its study.

Focusing on the history of scholarship, then, I seek to epitomize the study of an absence. Why is it that 19th-century religious scholarship neglected the comparative study of Judaism, Christianity, and Islam – a form of study that it had inherited from a long tradition? It is true that 19th-century historicism sought to see phenomena as rooted in their cultural and historical context and to give each nation its due, as Ranke noted. Still, comparative scholarship blossomed, in various fields, in the last decades of the century, at the acme of British imperial power. In a number of ways, the colonial enterprise fostered a comparative approach – with the avowed view of claiming the supremacy of European culture over that of other civilizations. The inquiry also stands at the confluence of different disciplines blooming in our period, in particular the study of Islam on the one hand (together with Arabic, Turkic, and Iranian philology) and Jewish Studies (or rather the Wissenschaft des Judentums) on the other hand.[22]

Jewish scholars played a specific role in the emergence of the history of religion, at the crossroads with Orientalism, in the second half of the 19th century. This role reflects their peculiar status and self-perception, as well as a unique aspect of the discipline. By and large, among European scholars of religion, only the Jews did not identify as Christians, at least culturally. Jewish scholars sought at once, in different ways, to achieve various goals, not always compatible with one another. They sought to apply philological and historical methods to Jewish texts and documents which they considered unduly ignored or misunderstood by Christian scholars. Moreover, moved as they were at once by a sense of belonging to their own traditional Jewish culture and by their intense desire to become full-fledged members of society at large, they believed that, as Orientals living in the West, they could offer a bridge of sorts between the cultures and languages of Asia and Europe.

The rise of Romanticism and of national movements contributed to the break-up of the integrative reflection on the three great monotheist traditions we now call the Abrahamic religions. This break-up was finalized by the combined impact of a traditional contempt for Islam and a patronizing (or worse) attitude to contemporary Muslim societies.[23]

---

[22] See for instance Christian Wiese, *Challenging Colonial Discourse. Jewish Studies and Protestant Theology in Wilhelmine Germany*. Leiden/Boston: Brill 2005.

[23] A similar phenomenon can also be observed about religions and societies of black Africa, as demonstrated by David Chidester, *Empire of Religion. Imperialism and Comparative Religion*. Chicago/London: Chicago University Press 2014.

Side by side with this aversion to Islam, the new racial anti-Semitism was growing. At the time, the Jews of Europe were starting to leave the ghettos and enter Western European societies – a dramatic change of the old patterns of relationship between Christians and Jews during many centuries. With their new economic integration in society at large, however, the Jews soon discovered, painfully, that this was not enough to earn them what Heine called an 'entrance ticket' to European society – a ticket which only baptism could really provide. The Jews, as already mentioned, were perceived as stemming from the Orient and often considered as still belonging to it. It should be noted that Jews often embraced these oriental roots with pride. This self-identification is reflected in the Orientalizing architecture of many 19th century synagogues, a style meant to allude to the mythical symbiosis, or *convivencia*, between Muslims, Jews, and Christians in al-Andalus, medieval Islamic Spain.[24]

The scholarly study of Christianity (in particular early and late antique Christianity) which slowly sought to disengage itself from theology (without ever fully succeeding in achieving this goal) represents a special case in the emerging comparative and historical study of religions. The appearance, in the last three decades of the 19th century, of the new concept of 'world religions' broke the traditional family relationship of Judaism, Christianity, and Islam, as it insisted in seeing Christianity to be a full-fledged universalist religion, while Islam was granted this status only grudgingly, and Judaism rejected into the category of racially and ethnically determined religions.[25]

The history of scholarship represents more than the list of the achievements of individual scholars; it is also made of scholarly institutions, in the framework of which free research and intellectual breakthroughs can happen. Such scholarly institutions include universities but also theological seminaries, scientific academies, scholarly journals, conferences, and publishing venues, and companies. In contradistinction to early modernity, when scholarship remained essentially the personal adventure of highly gifted and idiosyncratic individuals, from the 19th century on, research has mainly been carried on within universities. It is, indeed, the dialectical interaction between individual thinking and institutionalized systems of knowledge that transforms disciplines. One cannot really understand intellectual discourse and scholarly practices without constant reference to their cultural, religious, and ideological background.

---

24 See for instance the discussion of this theme in John Efron, *German Jewry and the Allure of the Sefardic*. Princeton/Oxford: Princeton University Press 2016. This embrace of the Orient would be echoed in the Zionist urge to return to the East, to Palestine. At the turn of the century, art in Jewish Palestine, too, would embrace the Orientalizing trend.

25 See Guy G. Stroumsa, *The Idea of Semitic Monotheism*, Chapter 9.

Since their birth in the 17th century, the modern humanistic disciplines, like the natural sciences, have been fascinated by comparison. The comparison between languages, cultures, legal systems, scientific traditions, mythologies, and societies, however, has always reflected an effort in detecting differences as much as in seeking similarities between them. These early modern humanistic disciplines were the offspring of the puzzlement generated by the new cultures and societies revealed by the great discoveries. The comparative element gathered momentum in the 19th century, starting with linguistics, under the impact of Franz Bopp's seminal studies on the grammar of the Indo-European languages, and reached its zenith toward the end of that century.[26]

Comparison lies at the center of the non-theological study of religions since the 18th century. Ever present, and indispensable, comparison is always highly problematic as a method. It is rarely innocent.[27] It is also a constant exercise, one that is at the core of experimental investigation. What do we do when we compare? The answer depends, of course, upon one's goals, viewpoint, and culture. Anthropologists, in particular, have reflected much on the question of comparison between societies, both those broadly similar and those highly different from one another.[28]

---

26 See further, Stroumsa, *Semitic Monotheism*, Chapter 9.
27 Bruce Lincoln, Theses on Comparison, in: Bruce Lincoln, *Apples and Oranges. Explorations In, On, and With Comparison*. Chicago/London: Chicago University Press 2018, 25–33, esp. 25. See also, in the same volume, *The Future of History of Religions*, 14–24 (written together with Cristiano Grottanelli). David Chidester, *Empire of Religion. Imperialism and Comparative Religion*. Chicago/London: Chicago University Press 2014. Chidester shows how British Imperialism in the second half of the 19th century used taxonomies of religions in order to support its colonial conquests in South Africa. See already David Chidester, *Savage Systems. Colonialism and Comparative Religion in Southern Africa*. Charlottesville/London: University Press of Virginia 1996. On comparison in the study of ancient religions, see Claude Calame/Bruce Lincoln (eds.), *Comparer en histoire des religions antiques*. Liège: Presses universitaires de Liège 2012. For the wise remarks of a Western Medievalist puzzled by what she sees in India, see Caroline Bynum, Avoiding the Tyranny of Morphology; Or, Why Compare?, in: *History of Religions* 53 (2014), 341–368. For an attempt to negotiate a path between too much and too little comparison in the study of religion, see Wendy Doniger, *The Implied Spider. Politics and Theology in Myth*. New York: Columbia University Press 1998, 64–71.
28 About comparison as experimental method, see Philippe Borgeaud, *L'histoire des religions*. Gollion: Infolio 2013, 182–185. For a rich volume of studies on comparatism by historians and anthropologists alike, see Renaud Gagné/Simon Goldhill/Geoffrey E. R. Lloyd (eds.), *Regimes of Comparatism: Frameworks of Comparison in History, Religion and Anthropology* (Jerusalem Studies in Religion and Culture 24). Leiden/Boston: Brill 2018. For an analysis of the different kinds of comparatism in anthropology, see in particular in the volume, Philippe Descola, Anthropological Comparatisms: Generalisation, Symmetrisation, Bifurcation, 402–417. In 2019, Descola dedicated his last year of teaching at the Collège de France to the question of comparatism in anthropology. In the footsteps of E. E. Evans-Pritchard, he insists on the fact that comparison is the very essence of an-

Contemporary historiography of our discipline typically focuses on Protestant countries in the second half of the 19th century. Philippe Borgeaud, for instance, puts his finger on a climate of secularization in Protestant countries in the 1870s, while Hans Kippenberg follows the traditional emphasis on Protestant scholarship.[29] Until the early 20th century, the Catholic hierarchy was still fiercely fighting the critical methods in the study of the Scriptures, and Catholic theological faculties remained, by and large, unwilling to study religious phenomena and history in a modern, non-traditional way. Despite various daring attempts, such as those of the Dominicans of the École Biblique in Jerusalem since the days of Marie-Joseph Lagrange, O.P., Catholic scholars were prohibited from practicing higher criticism until Vatican II.

More precisely, it was within Protestant theological faculties in Germany that the new critical approach to the Scriptures was born, and that the progressive theological liberalization was most conspicuous, permitting the study of non-Christian religions, past and present. Fresh scholarly biblical hermeneutics eventually opened the way to the comparative study of religious texts from both the Ancient Near East and the Greco-Roman Mediterranean – a trend famously illustrated by the Göttingen *Religionsgeschichtliche Schule* in the last decade of the 19th century.[30] These ancient texts were now understood as reflecting the background, or *Sitz im Leben*, of the religious ideas expressed in the books of the Old and New Testament.

The obvious and massive cleft between Protestant and Catholic biblical scholarship, however, is also responsible for a common error of perception, when it is too often assumed that the 19th-century study of religion is essentially a Protestant affair. The combined evidence, showing the major importance of the transmission of knowledge between different European countries, and the crucial significance

---

thropology and seeks to distinguish between different kinds of comparatism. In this context, it is significant that, like the study of religion, modern anthropology dates from the last decades of the 19th century. In his 'Marett Lecture' (1950), Evans-Prichard had already argued that anthropology should be perceived as a kind of history, and that it belonged to the Humanities. See Edward Evan Evans-Pritchard, Social Anthropology. Past and Present, in: Edward Evan Evans-Pritchard, *Social Anthropology and Other Essays*. New York: The Free Press 1962, 139–154, esp. 152–154.

29 Philippe Borgeaud, *L'histoire des religions*, 134. Kippenberg's *Discovering Religious History in the Modern Age*, and is also true for those works calling attention to the high price paid by those reading religious history through confessional glasses. On this issue, Jonathan Z. Smith has shown in his seminal *Drudgery Divine* how much Protestant beliefs had impacted the study of early Christianity in its Hellenistic background. *Mutatis mutandis*, a similar argument could be made about ancient Israel and Near Eastern religions.

30 On the *Religionsgeschichtliche Schule*, see Gerd Lüdemann (ed.), *Die ‚Religionsgeschichtliche Schule'. Facetten eines theologischen Umbruchs*. Frankfurt/New York: Peter Lang 1996. See Chapter Eight below.

for the science of religion of ethnological studies, coming at the time mainly from Catholic missionaries, clearly discards such a misperception. It is as a complex combination of elements coming from different cultural and intellectual traditions that the modern study of religion emerged.[31]

In the trajectory of modern scholarship on religion, a number of significant shifts in systems of knowledge brought to the reconstruction of central cognitive structures. The formation and re-structuring of concepts and methods modifies fields of study, sometimes profoundly transforming them. Such fields are ultimately related to the construction of the self, in particular when they deal directly with religious identities. In a time of profound and extensive secularization of European societies, the historical and comparative study of religions, which is a particularly delicate and interdisciplinary field of scholarship, has had a significant impact on both the transmission of knowledge and the transformation of European identities.

What was true in the 19th century remains true today. We witness, throughout Europe, bursts of Islamophobia and an animated, enduring, often strident, and sometimes violent public discussion about the ethnic, cultural, and religious implications of the massive immigration from Muslim countries, coming together with a worrisome renewal, under various garbs, of a Judaeophobia we naively thought was on the waning.[32]

Even the largely post-Christian Europe of the 21st century, indeed, does not seem to be quite done with its old obsessions about Muslims and Jews.

---

[31] I reached a similar conclusion about the early modern study of religion, in the 17th century, in *A New Science*.

[32] For a number of reasons, the use of 'Semite' and 'Semitic' has continued to be deeply ambivalent, and to this day, is often problematic. 'Anti-Semitism', as we know, is a term coined in the early 1880s, by the German journalist Wilhelm Marr, naming the political movement opposing the integration of Jews into society. Although this misnomer has retained its original connotations to this day, it is often argued that Arabs cannot be accused of Antisemitism in the sense of Judeophobia, since they too are Semites. This is of course a very weak syllogism, as has been demonstrated many times. Another claim, more relevant to our present inquiry, was levelled by Edward Said, when he argued that the popular anti-Semitic animus was transferred from a Jewish to an Arab target, and that this transference was made smoothly since the figure was essentially the same (i.e., the Arabs too are Semites, and therefore the same word can be used against them too). This is a specious argument, as cogently argued by Bernard Lewis in his *Semites and Anti-Semites*. New York/London: Norton 1986. The word itself, anti-Semitism, dates from the late 19th century, while according to Said, Orientalist anti-Arab animus is a much earlier phenomenon. Moreover, anti-Jewish animus never weakened, let alone disappeared, even with the growth of what is now called Islamophobia. Neither the word 'anti-Semitism' nor the hatred it refers to can be said to have been transferred from Jew to Arab. On this, see Gil Anidjar, *Semites. Race, Religion, Literature*. Stanford: Stanford University Press 2008, 13–38.

Azza Karam
Complimenting the Divine: The Multireligious as the Poetics of Resilience

> Three things are necessary for the salvation of man; to know what he ought to believe, to know what he ought to desire, and to know what he ought to do.
> – St. Thomas Aquinas

> Man is made by his belief as he believes, so he is.
> – Johann Wolfgang von Goethe

1 Introduction

One of the basic principles of the charter of the United Nations – an institution I served for nearly two decades – and I very strongly believe in, is that of the the dignity and equality of all human beings. All members of the United Nations – the governments – have pledged themselves to take joint and separate action with cooperation to maintain and encourage universal respect for and the observance of human rights and fundamental freedoms for all, without distinctions of race, sex, language, religion, ethnicity, nothing.

The Universal Declaration of Human Rights and the International Covenant on Human Rights proclaim the principles of nondiscrimination and equality before the law and include the right to freedom of thought, conscience, or belief. Furthermore, the Declaration on the Elimination of all Forms of Intolerance and Discrimination Based on Religion or Belief, notes, among other things, and I quote:

> the disregard and infringement of human rights and fundamental freedoms in particular to the freedom of thought, conscience, religion, or whatever belief, have brought directly or indirectly wars and great suffering to humankind, especially where they serve as a means of foreign interference in the internal affairs of other states and amount to kindling hatred between peoples and nations.[1]

---

[1] Declaration on the Elimination of All Forms of Intolerance and of Discrimination Based on Religion or Belief, on: UN Human Rights Office (25.11.1981), URL: https://www.ohchr.org/en/instruments-mechanisms/instruments/declaration-elimination-all-forms-intolerance-and-discrimination (03.2.2023).

Open Access. © 2023 Azza Karam, published by De Gruyter. This work is licensed under the Creative Commons Attribution 4.0 International License.
https://doi.org/10.1515/9783111241463-006

We are living in very odd times indeed, and I do not just mean Covid times, as well as the climate changes that we are all experiencing in every single corner of the world. Both of these are already effectively changing us slowly but surely in ways, we may yet to appreciate. In the introduction, we heard about how this way of congregating virtually and of conversing has already become our the normal. Surely, this way of being together – and yet not really *being* together – will impact our perception of one another – at the minimum, it will even impact how we feel about the way that we present ourselves, to whom we present, to whom we talk.

It is difficult not to take into consideration whether I am talking to myself or if I am talking to others and to ask myself who these people are that I am talking to but which I can only see through this screen. The fact is, that even asking myself these questions, in and of itself, will have an impact on what I choose to say, and how I choose to say it. This, in turn, also relates to how we see ourselves and how we appreciate those 'with us' – or those not with us. This brings out in very stark ways some good things, but also perhaps some not very good things. I refer to it as the poverty of goodness and the goodness of poverty.

We live in times of what many describe as a democratic recession. A world, in which uttering words of hatred to those who are unlike us, is increasingly normalized, and in some cases, speaking ill of the other is even seen as 'a good thing'. This absence of what some of us would think of as common decency, belongs to what I consider what I consider part of a democratic deficit. And if this deficit is to be reversed, it will take a very deliberate effort by each and everyone of us – individuals, communities, and institutions. I argue that this is very much needed, because we need to expand the shrinking space for dissent and for pluralism, but we must also make sure, we do so in a way that makes the dissent civil, not warlike.

All the more ironic then, that, when it comes to promoting human rights, the foreign policies of some governments (particularly Western ones) tend to single out specific aspects of religious realities – if they speak to religion at all. The acknowledgement of religion comes through the lens of religious freedom or freedom of expression – perhaps initially inspired by the concerns for Christian minorities elsewhere in the world. Many foreign policy makers in Europe in particular but also the United States, are in the process of creating several bodies which are attempting to have a role in promoting freedom of religion on the global stage. They do this in many ways, including shining a light on the persecution of religious minorities and prisoners of conscience, calling for and aiding efforts to abolish blasphemy bans, and sometimes also selective naming and shaming of countries in violation of freedom of religion. This is important, but remains very much a Western Hemisphere-led effort (largely European and North American).

Yet, and this is an important qualification, many scholars as well as peacemakers and development practitioners, argue that there are limits to what can be accomplished by a narrow focus on religious freedom. Having the right to worship according to the dictates of one's conscience actually does not automatically translate into contexts of political pluralism and support for civic engagement and freedom of expression. The focus on freedom of religion may, in fact, either exclude or marginalize an equally necessary focus on the freedoms of those championing democracy, human rights, anti-corruption, and environmental concerns. Creating separate governmental commissions or intergovernmental entities focusing on diverse parts of human rights means, we may not connect the dots and thus end up with neither a 'whole of government' approach nor a 'whole of society' understanding.

So, as we increase the focus on religious freedom, we must ask ourselves whether we also potentially diminish the focus on the role of faith in motivating and inspiring and playing both a leading key and instigative role to champion democracy and human rights. If these features – i.e. intersecting and interconnected human rights, anti-corruption, environmental concerns among other dynamics – are not simultaneously also actively struggled for, are we potentially 'allowing' political regimes, whose environmental policies are problematic, and who repress opposition and dissent on other matters of human rights, to still be patted on the back because they pass legislations which protects certain religious minorities, even if some of these minorities are themselves oppressing their own members (e.g. women or LGBTIQ groups)?

The fact is, it is actually possible for some authoritarian states to embrace religious freedom, while the freedom to express dissent constitutes an existential threat to them. This prompts an important inquiry based on where we sit in Religions for Peace[2]. This is where all faith communities – all religious institutions – are governing members, committed to upholding the values common to all faiths (including love, compassion, mercy), and serving the common good – together. Imagine: What would happen if these very same religious leaders and institutions commit to working together, in all parts of the world where they coexist, to secure freedom of thought, freedom of conscience, freedom of religion and belief – for one another's communities and institutions?

---

2 Religions for Peace is often seen as the 'United Nations of religions', in the same way that the United Nations is composed of government, or political institutions, as members, *Religions for Peace* is composed of religious institutions and representatives of faith communities around the world, as its members.

2 Freedom

But wait, before we seek to imagine these changes, let us first arrive at some kind of a common understanding of what 'freedom' could mean. What are the poetics of freedom, as I understand them, especially, where they intersect with thought, conscience, and belief?

Nelson Mandela noted in his work The Long Walk to Freedom that,

> [T]here is no easy walk to freedom anywhere and many of us will have to pass through the valley of the shadow of death. Again, and again before we reach the mountain top of our desires.[3]

The Rev. Martin Luther King Jr. is quoted to have said:

> [W]hen we allow freedom to ring, when we let it ring from every village and every hamlet, from every state and every city, we will be able to speed up that day when all of God's children, black men and white men, Jews and gentiles, Protestants and Catholics will be able to join hands and sing the words of the old negro spiritual, 'free at last, free at last, thank God almighty we are free at last'.[4]

Rather than explore the entire gambit of what freedom entails to so many and every individual, allow me to settle for a very quick look at how the notion of freedom is sometimes understood and practiced in terms of sustainable development or the sustainable development goals – referred to as Agenda 2030. But why do I choose to look at freedom through the sustainable development goals? Because whether we realize it or not, the Sustainable Development Goals were actually arrived at and signed by 193 governments, the members of the United Nations. For those of you who know the challenges of international human rights and international humanitarian law, for those of you very familiar with the challenges of having even one government agree to one policy direction, there is little doubt that you should be able to appreciate what it means to have 193 governments agree to a set of global priorities for human development. It is a very significant undertaking. All the more so in the context of a very divided and divisive set of realities around us today.

---

[3] The words of Nelson Mandela echo through the decades, in: Los Angeles Times (06.12.2013), URL: https://www.latimes.com/world/worldnow/la-fg-wn-nelson-mandela-dies-famous-quotes-story.html (03.02.2023).

[4] Beyond black-and-white: Essential moments from MLK's historic 'I have a dream speech', on: NBC News (28.08.2013), URL: https://www.nbcnews.com/news/photo/beyond-black-white-essential-moments-mlks-historic-i-have-dream-flna8c11024425 (03.02.2023).

So, let us visit – briefly – freedom as development, or development itself as freedom. Unsurprisingly, I will refer to Professor Amartya Sen – an Indian economist who was awarded the 1998 Nobel Peace Prize in economic sciences for his contributions to welfare economics and social choice theory and for his interests in the problems of societies poorest members. Professor Sen himself, in his exegesis of *Development As Freedom*, quotes an 18th century poet, William Cowper, on freedom:

> Freedom has a thousand charms to show [...] that slaves, however contented, never know.[5]

Sen explains how, in a world of unprecedented increases and overall opulence, millions of people living in rich and poor countries are still unfree. Even if they are not technically slaves, they are denied elementary freedom and remained imprisoned in one way or another by economic poverty, social deprivation, political tyranny, or cultural authoritarianism.

It is rather sad, that Sen was actually talking about the 1990s. Now consider what it is like in a Covid-riddled and climate aggrieved world, where some governments have found an excuse in stopping the transmission of the disease, to exercise even more authoritarian controls. A Covid-riddled world which has shone a very harsh light on the enormous inequalities of access to basic needs in our society, let alone access to necessary vaccines. The main purpose of development, Sen argued, was to 'spread freedom and its thousand charms to the unfree'. The unfree we know to be in today's figures, the millions who live not only in poverty, not only without access to affordable quality education, decent levels of food, basic nutrition, basic sanitation, a safe and secure environment but also without access to decent employment opportunities. In fact, the unfree are those whose lives are impacted simultaneously by the intersecting calamities of all of this plus an environment which is endangering each and every life of this planet.

Freedom, as Sen argues, is both a means and an end. He spoke of social institutions like markets, political parties, legislature, the judiciary, and the media as contributing to development by enhancing individual freedom. These institutions themselves are sustained by social values. Thus Sen links values, institutions, development, and freedom.

Using Sen's understanding then, and juxtaposing that understanding against today's environmental realities, we can say that freedom is the holistic work of ensuring that we have a sustainable environment which comes together with and enables the essentials of a dignified life. A life where access to the basic needs such

---

5 Amartya Sen, *Development As Freedom*. Oxford: Oxford University Press 1999, 298.

as quality education, nutrition and healthcare, and decent employment are enabled by the absence of all forms of violence and the prevalence of security; that is, a life of dignity. This underlines why it is important for institutions such as Religions for Peace to convene and enable religious institutions to work together to realise that freedom.

3 Freedom as Mercy

I choose to focus on the poetics of freedom from the prism of the values common to all faiths: mercy, love, and compassion.

So where is the link to freedom as mercy? In the Bhagavad Gita it says:

you are what you believe in, you become that which you believe you can become.[6]

So, if we believe in mercy, we shall become merciful. And in doing so make the world less cold and more just.

Let me ask a few rhetorical questions: Can we live without experiencing mercy ourselves? A sense of mercy towards ourselves? What about the sense of mercy towards and from one another? What kind of a life is it in which we do not experience that sense of mercy from one another and towards ourselves? If we cannot live without some form of mercy, should we not understand then, that within each of our faith traditions there is a call, a demand, an obligation, an imperative to be merciful towards others?

But how can we be merciful towards others if we deny them their right to exercise their freedom of religion or belief? How can we claim to be people of some faith if we do not actively struggle for that freedom, not only for ourselves, but for each and every fellow human being? As the Bhagavad Gita again enlightens, there is mercy in showing mercy, so it is merciful to demand this, as I claim the freedom to believe in the Divine in whatever form I believe that Divine takes. I will actively affirm your freedom to believe and to exercise that belief.

---

[6] Neha Borkar, 11 Bhagavad Gita Quotes By Lord Krishna on Life and Success That You Need To Know, on: Indiatimes (05.06.2020), URL: https://www.indiatimes.com/culture/who-we-are/11-simple-lessons-from-the-bhagavad-gita-that-are-all-you-need-to-know-about-life-244390.html (03.02.2023).

4 Freedom as Love

Now let me pivot to freedom as love of the Divine – and thus the love of one and all. There is an African proverb which says: 'tell me who you love, and I will tell you who you are.'

A Turkish-Muslim scholar, Dr. Adnan Oktar, elaborates on one of the verses of the Quran in which it is explicitly stated that God points to the existence of people from different faiths and opinions as His creations. I will not quote the Surah (verse) in full, but it is number 5 verse 84. The Surah basically says (and here I am paraphrasing the translation of Youssef Ali)[7] that the Quran is meant to confirm earlier scriptures, and is intended to guard the Truths in these earlier Scriptures. So we should refrain from judging between people, especially as each of us has 'been prescribed a law, and a way'. I am reminded here of the point Pope Francis' once raised and often (mis)quoted: 'who am I to judge?'. The Surah then goes on to make a point I find equally beautiful: That if God had so willed, he would have made us all a single people. Instead, he has given us choice, so we must strive to be more virtuous (also understood as honour God's commandments). What this means to me, as a Muslim, is a clear injunction to have inner love/compassion/mercy for people of all faiths, races, and nations, because these are all the creations of the Divine.

This is echoed in every single faith tradition. Of course, we can search to find the mean, nasty, horrid things. Or we can dwell on that which is calling for love. Let us move away from scripture for a second and let us look at Chinua Achebe, a Nigerian novelist, poet, professor, and critic. I quote him when he says:

> We cannot trample upon the humanity of others without devaluing our own.[8]

The Igbo put it concretely in their own proverb:

> He who will hold another down in the mud must stay in the mud to keep him down.

But we cannot stay in the mud. As people of faith, whatever, we are called upon, in the words of St. Teresa Avila, not only to love the Divine, to accustom ourselves to make many acts of love for they kindle, but also to melt the soul.

---

7 Cf. The Holy Qur'an online, Translation by A. Yusuf Ali, on: quranyusufali.com, URL: https://quranyusufali.com/ (03.02.2023).
8 Introduction on Chinua Achebe, on: goodreads.com, URL: https://www.goodreads.com/quotes/261567-we-cannot-trample-upon-the-humanity-of-others-without-devaluing#:~:text=%E2%80%9CWe%20cannot%20trample%20upon%20the%20humanity%20of%20others%20without%20devaluing,mud%20to%20keep%20him%20down.%E2%80%9D (03.02.2023).

So, taking into account holy scriptures, poetry, and sayings, we can detect a very humble reflection on the poetics of freedom: The freedom to love the Divine as reflected in each and every living thing – not just humans – is not a choice that we make, it is an obsession that we must have.

The love of the Divine is at once strengthened and tempered by the freedom to see the reflection of the Divine in each and every human being and living thing, including those who may not even believe in the Divine. Freedom is also compassion. In the Kopan Monastary in Nepal, Lama Thubten Zopa Rinpoche speaking in the 33rd Kopan course says, I quote:

> If our mind is devoid of compassion, if our heart is devoid of compassion, inner peace, and contentment, then no matter what extensive things or external practices we perform is not real, is not spiritual. Our heart is empty of spiritual practice.[9]

I repeat, in my words, without compassion, our heart is empty of spiritual practice.

Here is an outlook that is encapsulated by a poet, a novelist, a singer, a memoirist, Maya Angelou, who passed away in 2019. Her quote is:

> My mission in life is not merely to survive but to thrive, and to do so with some passion, some compassion, some humour, and some style.[10]

About time, we come to paying God a compliment. St. Theresa of Avila said: 'you pay God a compliment by asking great things of him.'[11] This is the vision of service in *Religions for Peace* – we aim to pay God one compliment after another, making one great demand after another. We ask God to help us realise the freedoms of all religions to make peace, to enable the realization with a humility based on an obsession with love, with mercy and with compassion. An obsession with the Divine in all of its manifestations and forms.

I want to quote the Buddha where he says:

---

9 Kyabje Lama Zopa Rinpoche, Compassion is the Essence of Religion, on: Lama Yeshe Wisdom Archive, URL: https://www.lamayeshe.com/article/compassion-essence-religion (03.02.2023).
10 Maya Angelou, on: Twitter (28.03.2021), URL: https://twitter.com/drmayaangelou/status/1376258471251836931?lang=en (03.02.2023).
11 St. Teresa of Ávila, You pay God a compliment by asking great things of him, on: catholicdigest.com, URL: https://www.catholicdigest.com/from-the-magazine/quiet-moment/st-teresa-of-avila-you-pay-god-a-compliment-by-asking-great-things-of-him/ (03.02.2023).

> Little though he recites the sacred texts, but puts the Teaching into practice, forsaking lust, hatred, and delusion, with true wisdom and emancipated mind, clinging to nothing of this or any other world — he indeed partakes of the blessings of a holy life.[12]

And this brings me to resilience. The meanings of resilience written in ecology, sociology and the studies of social ecological systems is effectively, and I am trying to cobble together from all these different disciplines, the focus on change in complex systems interacting, to define resilient as a desirable thing. But let us try to see resilience as connectivity to systems or communities. Resilience is rooted in and within complex interactions. It is about movement, change and transformation, so, resilience, therefore, is not about surviving as an individual, although, of course, it can include that. But in a world linked by Covid where no one is safe until everyone is, we are required to be resilient, by handling the collective 'we' faced with the multiple challenges.

For many, faith is where the resilience is to be found, not only because of what we believe individually, but perhaps also because of what our faith teaches us about understanding and living freedom as connecting with and connected to one another. I like to think that the freedom we viewed in the context of mercy, compassion, and love is both the means and the end of resilience. So, what does all this mean? Here, I quote my favorite poet and author, Kahlil Gibran (The Prophet):

> You give but little when you give of your possessions, it is when you give of yourself that you truly give.[13]

An existence, in which we have focused on our individual selves, our own institutions, our own nation state boundaries. An existence, in which we have given only to our immediate community, family, whichever close relation, is an existence, in which we have effectively asked very little indeed of God, actually. It does not sound to me that this would be the exercise of compassion, mercy or love. In fact, such an existence, in which we focus on the immediate or our own, that, which is like us, that kind of existence limits our freedom and may actually well curb our resilience. All of us, even if all of us were vaccinated in any given country, are still by no means safe. Covid has gone nowhere; it is still very much with us.

Therefore, confronted with Covid and its myriad impacts, Religions for Peace, learning from over 50 years of convening religious communities to work together, understands that our faiths together are the means of building an interconnected

---

12 Yamakavagga: Pairs. translated from the Pali by Acharya Buddharakkhita, on: accesstoinsight.org, URL: https://www.accesstoinsight.org/tipitaka/kn/dhp/dhp.01.budd.html#dhp-19 (03.02.2023).
13 Kahlil Gibran, On Giving, on: poets.org, URL: https://poets.org/poem/giving-0 (03.02.2023).

web of resilience for our humanity and our planet. We learned that, to focus on or only with one religious community, is actually to unravel the connectivity, which the virus itself was showing us. The virus does not distinguish between anyone or limits itself to any one nation, ethnicity, social status, gender, or any boundary. Rather the virus and its impacts are breaking through our walls of othering and disconnecting us further. The virus is a negative loop in our lives.

The positive loop is to build the resilience to realize our freedom as mercy, compassion, and love; to serve all faiths as an act of one's own faith. The positive loop is to secure the web of human and planetary connectivity, so that the multireligious – the multifaith – is the means to resilience and resilience is faced and built together, is the multifaith web of connectivity. In other words, asking God to help us realize that cohesion especially in these times, is paying God a compliment because it is asking great things of God. We ask great things of God, as we ask great things of one another; as we serve one another, regardless of our differences. Because we will never be safe within the parameters and boundaries that we think we have. If Covid and climate change have shown us anything, they have shown us that, in order for us to survive and to thrive, we are absolutely compelled to look after one another. It is not a choice, it is an imperative.

That is why Religions for Peace, the organization I am privileged to serve, within the first two weeks in March after the global lockdowns were starting, set up the Multireligious Humanitarian Fund. Why? It was not because religious organizations are not already working at warp speed delivering a thousand and one percent. In fact, every single religious community is working non-stop. Because we know that religious organizations actually are at the forefront of humanitarian efforts. Religious organisations are the first responders in most places around the world, whether that humanitarian crisis happens to be human-made or whether it happens to be a natural disaster, religious institutions are out there serving all the time. But what we noticed, very soon, was, that every single religious institution, every single first responder, was responding to serve everybody, but primarily through their own organizations – and for them. So, as the religious organisations are serving, but they serve pretty much on their own.

Religions for Peace's business is to seek that cycle of freedom, that requires – in fact, demands – mercy, compassion, and love towards others, through giving. And that is why we created a fund that is meant to support those efforts – and it is just starting on a small scale. We realise, that in different parts of the world, all are responding to the same needs, but we support those who are prepared to work together, Christian, Muslim, Jewish, Hindu, Buddhist, whatever the religious composition in any place, they are actually making a difference by working together, determined to serve together.

This is paying God a huge compliment. Because it is in the determination to give of our resources to the 'other'. That is what we are trying to build as resilience. If we succeed in enabling religious communities of whatever type to be working together in this moment of extended crisis, then, we are succeeding in building a framework of social cohesion. But if each religious institution continues to go alone, then no matter how many they serve, no matter how many countries they serve, we will still be talking about siloed forms of existence. Can we afford not to work together to build that mutual resilience that the virus and everything else around us is telling us what we absolutely need, because the survival of all depends on the survival of one?

We are at that moment in time, where we have to make a choice, not to be faithful only, not to decide to give to our own community only, but to decide to actively work together to give and share the resources that we have to serve one another. That is the ultimate test, of whether we have actually imbibed freedom for one and all, whether we have actually delivered on the basic tenants of our faith, whether we are actually building a resilience or simply coping for the time being, and whether we are going to build social cohesion or live fractured for the rest of the time that we have on this earth.

Contributors

Hans-Peter Grosshans holds the Chair of Systematic Theology at the University of Münster and is director of the Institute of Ecumenical Theology of the Faculty of Protestant Theology at Münster university (Germany). From 2020 – 2021 he was President and since 2022 he is Vice-President of the European Academy of Religion.

Azza Karam serves as the Secretary General of Religions for Peace (New York, US). She holds a Professorship of Religion and Development at the Vrije Universiteit in Amsterdam. Dr. Karam currently is a member of the United Nations Secretary General's 'High Level Advisory Board on Effective Multilateralism'.

Vassilis Saroglou is Professor of Psychology at the UCL-University of Louvain (Belgium). His research areas include the psychology of religion, personality, social, and cross-cultural psychology, moral psychology, and psychology of positive emotions. He has developed long-term empirical research on theoretically and socially critical issues regarding religion, spirituality, fundamentalism, and atheism.

Guy G. Stroumsa is Martin Buber Professor Emeritus of Comparative Religion at The Hebrew University of Jerusalem (Israel) and Professor Emeritus of the Study of the Abrahamic Religions and Emeritus Fellow of Lady Margaret Hall, University of Oxford. He is a member of the Israel Academy of Sciences and Humanities since 2008.

Rowan Williams was Archbishop of Canterbury from 2002 to 2012, the 35th Master of Magdalene College from 2013–2020, and is Honorary Professor of Contemporary Christian Thought at the University of Cambridge (UK). He is the author of numerous theological and spiritual books and scholarly articles.

Judith Wolfe is Professor of Philosophical Theology at the University of St Andrews' School of Divinity (UK), where she researches and teaches in systematic and philosophical theology, as well as in theology and the arts. She serves internationally on grant-funded projects, advisory and editorial boards in these areas, and is also a senior research fellow of Blackfriars Hall, Oxford, and a professorial fellow of Australian Catholic University.

Index of Persons

Achebe, Chinua 83
Achterberg, Peter 50
Ali, Youssef 83
Angelou, Maya 84
Anidjar, Gil 76
Aquinas, Thomas 34, 77
Arnold, Matthew 27, 28
Arvidsson, Stefan 67
Augustine 7, 65
Avila, Theresa 83, 84
Batson, C. Daniel 43, 46
Benedict XVI 7
Bernal, Martin 68, 69
Berthold-Bond, Daniel 33
Bertrand, Louis 66
Bleidorn, Wiebke 53
Blumenberg, Hans 68
Bopp, Franz 74
Borgeaud, Philippe 71, 74, 75
Borkar, Neha 82
Bourdieu, Pierre 68
Braude, Benjamin 65
Brewer, Marilynn B. 49
Bucher, Anton 53
Buddha 84
Buddharakkhita, Acharya 85
Bynum, Caroline 74
Calame, Claude 74
Carpenter, Tom 43
Chadwick, Owen 68
Chidester, David 72, 74
Collier, Paul 16
Collins, Haper 20
Comte, Auguste 68
Cowper, William 81
Dawkins, Richard 28
Deconchy, Jean-Pierre 41
Delpierre, Vanessa 56
Dent, Eric B. 54
Dernelle, Rebecca 56
Descola, Philippe 74
Dillon, Michele 40, 53, 55
Doebler, Stefanie 44
Doniger, Wendy 74

Efron, John 73
Ekici, Tufan 44
Eliot, Thomas S. 6
Epiphanius of Salamis 65
Esses, Victoria M. 46
Evans-Pritchard, Edward Evan 74, 75
Farina, Dan 40, 53, 55
Fichte, Johann Gottlieb 25
Freud, Sigmund 72
Furnham, Aadrian 59
Gadamer, Hans-Georg 5, 6, 7, 8, 14
Gagné, Renaud 74
Gallie, Walter B. 14
Galliford, Natasha 59
Galloway, Susan 54
Gatrell, Peter 16
Gebauer, Jochen E. 54
Gibran, Kahlil 85
Goethe, Johann Wolfgang von 77
Goldenberg, David M. 66
Goldhill, Simon 74
Goldziher, Ignaz 66
Gorringe, Timothy 20
Grabar, Oleg 70
Grosshans, Hans-Peter 63, 89
Grossmann, Igor 49
Grottanelli, Cristiano 74
Guardini, Romano 26
Habermas, Jürgen 8, 9, 10, 12, 18
Haggard, Megan 43
Haldane, John 5, 6, 22
Hall, Deborah 43
Hazard, Paul 69
Hegel, Georg Wilhelm Friedrich 25, 31, 32, 33, 68
Heidegger, Martin 26, 29, 30, 31, 32
Herder, Johann Gottfried 70
Hibbing, John R. 53
Hodson, Gordon 46
Hoffarth, Mark Romeo 46
Hopwood, Christopher J. 53
Houtman, Dick 50
How, Alan 8
Inglehart, Ronald 49, 56
Irwin, Robert 70

Index of Persons

Jackson, Joshua C. 39
Jackson, Lynne M. 46
Jasinskaja-Lahti, Inga 59
Jetten, Jolanda 59
John of Damascus 65
Jones, William 65
Jost, John T. 54
Kahneman, Daniel 63
Kant, Immanuel 31, 32, 33
King, Martin Luther (Jr.) 80
Kippenberg, Hans 75
Kojeve, Alexandre 33
Lagrange, Marie-Joseph 75
Lao, Joseph R. 54
Lee, Kibeom 54
Leonardelli, Geoffrey J. 49
Lewis, Bernard 70, 76
Lewis, Clive S. 20, 21, 26
Lincoln, Bruce 74
Lloyd, Geoffrey E. R. 74
Łowicki, Paweł 58
Löwith, Karl 30
Lüdemann, Gerd 75
MacIntyre, Alasdair 7, 10, 11, 14, 23
Mandela, Nelson 80
Marr, Wilhelm 76
Marx, Karl 31
Massa, Francesco 64
Matz, David 43
McCrae, Robert R. 52
Mendelson, Jack 8
Messling, Markus 69
Molnar, Danielle S. 46
Monod, Jean-Claude 68
Müller, Max 66
Nietzsche, Friedrich 9, 31
Norris, Pippa 49, 56
Oktar, Adnan 83
Olender, Maurice 66
Oreg, Shaul 54
Orsi, Robert 71
Oser, Fritz K. 53
Pabst, Adrian 19
Pennycook, Gordon 58
Peterson, Erik 32
Peterson, Jonathan C. 53
Pickett, Cynthia L. 49
Quinet, Edgar 68, 70
Ranke, Leopold von 25, 72
Reinach, Salomon 66
Renan, Ernest 63, 66
Ribberink, Egbert 50
Ricœur, Paul 7, 8, 9, 10, 11, 12, 13, 14, 18, 19, 21, 22
Rinpoche, Kyabje Lama Zopa 84
Rose, Gillian 10
Rosen, Stanley 33
Rowatt, Wade C. 43
Said, Edward 70, 71, 76
Sandel, Michael 12, 19
Santos, Henri C. 49
Saroglou, Vassilis 3, 40, 42, 43, 45, 46, 50, 53, 56, 89
Scarlett, W. George 53
Schall, James V. 7
Schlag, Martin 20
Schoenrade, Patricia 43
Schwab, Raymond 70
Selden, John 69
Sen, Amartya 81
Shatz, Adam 71
Sheehan, Jonathan 68
Siedentop, Larry 19
Smith, Jonathan Z. 71, 75
Smith, Kevin B. 53
St. Athanasius 34
Strauss, Friedrich David 68
Stroumsa, Guy G. 3, 63, 65, 69, 73, 74, 89
Sutin, Angelina R. 52
Taubes, Jacob 30
Tolkien, John R.R. 26
Tunzelmann, Alex von 17
Varnum, Michael E.W. 49
Ventis, W. Larry 43
Vincent, Ben 14
Ward, Michael 20
Wiese, Christian 72
Wink, Paul 40, 53, 55
Wittgenstein, Ludwig 5, 65
Wolfe, Judith 3, 32, 89
Wood, Wendy 43
Yangazoglou, Stavros 55
Young, Jason 54
Yucel, Deniz 44
Zimmermann, Jens 20, 22

www.ingramcontent.com/pod-product-compliance
Lightning Source LLC
Chambersburg PA
CBHW020130010526
44115CB00008B/1056